PACIFIC COAST CRABS AND SHRIMPS

by
Gregory C. Jensen, Ph.D.

D1361116

SEA CHALLENGERS • MONTEREY, CALIFORNIA

1995

A SEA CHALLENGERS PUBLICATION

Technical Editor: Dr. Mary K. Wicksten

Copy Editor: Ken Hashagen
second printing

Front Cover

Butterfly crab	*Cryptolithodes typicus* (upper left)
Widehand hermit	*Elassochirus tenuimanus* (lower left)
Candy stripe shrimp	*Lebbeus grandimanus* (right)

Cover photographs by the author

Library of Congress Cataloging-in-Publication Data

Jensen, Gregory C., 1957 -
    Pacific Coast crabs and shrimps / by Gregory C. Jensen.
        p. cm.
    Includes bibliographical references (p. 81) and index.
    ISBN 0-930118-20-0
    1. Crabs–Pacific Coast (North America) 2. Shrimps–Pacific Coast (North America)
    3. Crabs–Pacific Coast (North America) –Identification. 4. Shrimps–Pacific Coast
    (North America) –Identification. I. Title.
    QL444.M33J46 1995   94-39292
    595.3'842'0979–dc20   CIP

SEA CHALLENGERS

4 Sommerset Rise • Monterey, CA 93940
Printed in Hong Kong through Inter Print
Petaluma, CA U.S.A.
Typography and prepress production by Colorgraphics, Monterey, CA, U.S.A.

PREFACE

Study of life at the seashore, and also of life beneath the waves, is an absorbing and satisfying endeavor for many laymen, and of course for professional biologists. The graceful form and striking colors of the inhabitants of the ocean engage our eyes and aesthetic sensibilities. The interesting behaviors of the animals, furthermore, puzzle us, begging for explanation and persistent observation.

The book in your hands deals with one large and important group of animals, the decapod crustaceans. This particular assemblage includes shrimps, crabs, and lobsters, many of which are of great economic importance. But it also includes a wide variety of other crustaceans, mostly limited to the seas, that share the same general characteristics. One of these is the possession of five pairs of jointed appendages that are conventionally called legs. It is upon this ten-legged feature that the name decapod is based.

Nearly every marine habitat, between or below tide marks, will have one or more decapods. These crustaceans – especially crabs and hermit crabs – are usually common on rocky shores. And there are decapods on wave-swept sandy beaches and in mudflats of quiet bays. Many species are characteristic of subtidal habitats and of the open sea. Each kind has particular environmental requirements – an appropriate salinity, temperature, substratum, and food supply. What different decapods eat ranges from other animals, living or dead, down to seaweeds and tiny bits of detritus. Taken together, these crustaceans account for much of the turnover of organic compounds that goes on in the sea.

Greg Jensen's book includes over 160 of the species of decapods found between Alaska and Mexico and occurring at the shore or within a few miles of shore. He has pulled together information about all of them, and gives it to us in an accessible, easily understood format. Much of what he tells us is based on his own observations of these animals. Features used for identification of each species are accompanied by a brief account of the geographic range, habitat, diet, behavior, and other aspects of its biology. All of this information will be of interest to those who wish to understand the roles of decapods as carnivores, herbivores, or scavengers, and to appreciate how they are specialized for living where they do. One aim of Greg's work is to encourage us to protect these animals and to treat them with the respect they deserve.

The keys provided for identifying species and for distinguishing the several subgroups of decapods are instructive and do not depend on a lot of complicated jargon. They are – excuse me for introducing an overworked term – "user-friendly". The excellent illustrations will either clinch your identification or tell you that you need to start over or find the place where you took the wrong turn. In many cases, simply perusing the illustrations will enable you to hit the bull's-eye. Greg has photographed most of our decapods in their natural habitats, and is thus able to show us color patterns and other features that are extremely helpful in recognition of some species.

Greg hopes there aren't any mistakes in this book, on which he has worked diligently and with tremendous dedication. He will, nevertheless, be extremely grateful if you discern a problem or have some constructive criticisms. I am indebted to him for letting me read representative portions of this guide in advance of its publication. I recommend it to you with pleasure and confidence.

Eugene N. Kozloff
Friday Harbor, Washington

VANCOUVER ISLAND CRABS.

Fig. 1. Petalocerus bicornis.   Fig. 4. Platycarcinus recurvidens.
  „ 2. Chlorodius imbricatus.   „ 5. Oregonia longimana.
  „ 3. Pugettia Lordii.   „ 6. Cryptolithodes altafissura.

**Plate from J.K. Lord's "The Naturalist on Vancouver Island and British Columbia" (1866).
Courtesy of Special Collections, University of Washington Libraries, Neg. #14750.**

iv

ACKNOWLEDGMENTS

Rather than digging through a thesaurus trying to come up with fifteen different ways to say "thank you", I want to list all those who made putting all this together so much easier and how they helped out in various ways. So, my most sincere thanks:

to Dr. Mary Wicksten, who provided lots of pointers on where to look for many of the southern California species and who served as technical editor;

to those who shared valuable information, observations, or hot tips on where to find a particular critter, particularly Roland Anderson of the Seattle Aquarium, Michael Kyte, and Brett Dumbauld and Don Rothaus of the Washington Dept. of Fisheries. Andrew Cohen provided information on introduced species in San Francisco Bay, and Chuck Rawlinson of Depth Perceptions dive shop in Morro Bay directed us to particularly productive spots. Kris Feldman, Eileen Visser, Jonathon Stillman, Shane Anderson, and Art Denati of the Loch Lohmed Bait Shop all supplied much needed specimens;

to Dr. Eugene Kozloff for graciously agreeing to write the preface;

to Lynn and Ken Collins for letting us repeatedly use their home as a base of operations during our trips down south, as did John and Rob Catron and Keith Fenimore on our last trip. Tim Rawlings and Graeme Taylor helped out on our ventures into the Great White North, along with the staff of the Bamfield Marine Station;

to Patricia Coburn for her continuing encouragement and many insights into the publishing business, and to Leonard Feldman for his contract advice;

to Dr. David Armstrong, who provided the computer, lab, and office space used during this project;

to those who generously provided photographs: Drs. Jenifer Dugan and David Hubbard, Marc Chamberlain, and Mary Wicksten; also Doyne Kessler, Norbert Wu, Alex Kerstitch, and Daniel Gotshall;

to my summer REU students, Brian Badgely and Joy Jenkins, who served as guinea pigs to test the keys and who offered comments and suggestions;

to my diving partners Greg Williams, Dan Doty, Roland Anderson, and Dan Gotshall, and to Sam Sublett who went to heroic efforts to get us permission to dive at other locales.

But most of all, I want to thank Pamela Wardrup for sticking with me through all of the photo expeditions and particularly the long, cold night dives – patiently waiting while I took 'just one more' picture of some obscure little shrimp. This book would not have been possible without her help.

PHOTO CREDITS and TECHNIQUES

All photographs were taken by the author except for the following:
(species numbers in [brackets], followed by page number)

Marc Chamberlain [52] 34; [161] 79

Jenifer Dugan and David Hubbard [157] 77

Dan Gotshall [140] 71

Alex Kerstitch [47] 32

Mary Wicksten 12 (scanning electron micrograph); [126] 67

© Norbert Wu [163] 79

[152] 76 - from Schmitt, 1921

Most of the author's photographs were taken underwater with a Minolta X-700 camera in an Ikelite housing and using an Ikelite 150 strobe. These shots were predominantly taken with a 50 mm Minolta macro lens, but for very small subjects I used a Tamron 90 mm macro lens with a 2X converter to get images down to life-size while still maintaining a reasonable working distance from the subject. Aquarium shots were taken using the same camera with a small Minolta flash. Most images are on Fujichrome slide film (50 ASA), with a few on Kodachrome 25 or 64.

DEDICATION

I am pleased to dedicate this book to Paul Illg, Professor Emeritus of Zoology at the University of Washington, and to my parents, who tolerated the basement full of aquariums, mysterious packages in the freezer, and other hazards of being around a budding biologist.

Thirteenth century illustration of the sign Cancer, from the Prayerbook of Queen Mary.

TABLE OF CONTENTS

Introduction

The waters of the northeastern Pacific Ocean are home to a tremendous diversity of crabs and shrimps, varying in size from tiny pea crabs mere fractions of an inch across to massive king crabs with legs spanning five feet, and ranging from the highest tidal levels to the deepest abyss. Until now, identification of all but the most common of these animals has often been frustrating for the nonspecialist because most of the literature is either too technical, lacks illustrations, or is out of print. Although color patterns are extremely useful for identification of many species, these have been rarely mentioned and even less frequently illustrated. For example, many hermit crabs can be easily identified in the field based on the color of their claws and legs, even when partially retracted into their shell. But since most keys were constructed using faded, long-preserved specimens, they emphasize small spines and other structures that are often impossible to examine without both magnification and a considerable amount of stress for both of the parties involved.

This book is intended to simplify identification of the crabs, shrimps, and related crustaceans found from southeastern Alaska to the Mexican border. Many are shown here in color photographs for the first time and, as much as possible, I have used pictures taken in the field in order to convey some idea of their natural habitat. Emphasis has been placed on the species most likely to be encountered while diving or exploring tidepools so (with the exception of a few commercially-important shrimps) those that only occur at depths greater than 100 ft. have been omitted. In addition, many small, rarely collected species are also not included, especially those for which a color photograph would be of little or no use in identification. For these groups the interested reader should consult the references listed in the back of the book.

Although a cursory comparison of species lists will reveal a lower diversity of shrimps and crabs in our temperate waters than in the tropics, our region is especially rich in some groups such as hermit crabs, lithodid crabs, and hippolytid shrimp. More importantly, along much of our coast they are far more accessible and visible than in the tropics where (due to intensive predation pressure from fish) most only come out of hiding at night. With a little patience and a warm exposure suit the Pacific coast diver can observe many aspects of feeding, courtship, and other behaviors, and considering how little is known about most species, it is quite possible one can make valuable contributions to our knowledge of this interesting group.

Although it's safe to assume that searching for various kinds of crabs and shrimps will never approach the level of popularity that bird watching has achieved, there is much the same satisfaction in finding, identifying, and adding new species to your list of sightings. To this end, I have included a checklist following the index to help you keep track of the species you find. Ideally, one should keep a notebook or record in a dive log the location, depth, and date of the sightings, along with any notes on the habitat or unusual behaviors. I would greatly appreciate hearing of any sightings of animals outside of the ranges given in this book or other notable occurrences such as breeding aggregations. Send them to me c/o Sea Challengers, 4 Sommerset Rise, Monterey, California 93940.

Whether diving or exploring the intertidal, always obey the local regulations in regards to collecting and observe fishery size, sex, and seasonal limits when catching them for food. Minimum size regulations are not just arbitrary numbers designed to make life more difficult, but are instead intended to allow animals a chance to reproduce at least once before becoming available to the fishery. Even though many species are not covered by fisheries regulations (often because not enough is known about them to set limits), this shouldn't be taken as a license to collect anything that appears large enough to eat. In particular, long-lived, slow-growing species like the Puget Sound king crab and box crab (*Lopholithodes* spp.) are very susceptible to fishing pressure and have not been helped by the popular publications that encourage divers to collect them for food.

Keep in mind that as our steadily increasing population places increased demands on beaches and other natural areas, it is imperative that we each do our best to minimize the effects of our visits. When looking under rocks, always turn them back over to their original position while taking care not to crush the animals underneath. A good rule of thumb is not to flip over rocks that are too heavy for you to replace gently and under control. With proper care, our beaches can continue to offer the thrill of discovery for generations to come.

What is a crustacean?

Crustacea have been referred to as the "insects of the sea", a comparison many would rather not ponder as they sit down to enjoy a lobster or crab dinner. Yet the analogy is valid: just as their terrestrial counterparts are found in the air and on land throughout the world, the crustaceans have exploited virtually every part of the earth's seas. And while very few species of insects have ventured into marine habitats, the Crustacea have likewise had meager success in colonizing the land.

Like insects, crustaceans belong to the **Arthropoda** (meaning jointed-leg) along with spiders, scorpions, centipedes, and millipedes. Along with their jointed legs, the members of this group share such characters as an exoskeleton made of chitin, compound eyes, and a segmented body. Although the species of insects vastly outnumber all other arthropods combined, they show relatively little variation in body form, all having three pairs of legs, three major body divisions, and usually two pairs of wings. In contrast, the different groups within the Crustacea vary tremendously in the number of limbs and body divisions and some, like the barnacles, are so unusual as to be barely recognizable as crustaceans. With such a range of forms it is almost surprising that there are several unifying, consistent characters to distinguish this group from the rest of the arthropods. Crustaceans are the only group having two pairs of antennae. They also have a unique type of larva known as the nauplius (although most of the higher Crustacea pass through this stage while still in the egg and hatch in a more advanced form) and are the only living group with biramous limbs, meaning that each limb splits at the base to form two appendages. The outer appendage or exopod has been lost from the claws and walking legs of most of the higher Crustacea, but the basic biramous structure has been retained in the antennae, mouthparts, and abdominal appendages.

The major divisions of classification within the Crustacea are primarily based on the major 'divisions' of the body. The more primitive groups tend to have little differentiation between succeeding body segments, whereas the more derived ones have a much greater degree of specialization with different areas of the body performing different functions. All of the animals in this book fall within the largest and best known group within the Crustacea, known as the **Malacostraca**. In addition to shrimps and crabs, this group includes amphipods (e.g. "sand fleas"), isopods (including the terrestrial sow bugs and pill bugs), mysids (opossum shrimp), and other less familiar forms. Among the characters uniting this group are a total of 19 body segments (5 in the head, 8 thoracic, and 6 abdominal) with the female and male genital openings on the 6th and 8th thoracic segments, respectively.

With the exception of the stomatopods or mantis shrimps, all of the species dealt with here belong to the Order **Decapoda**. As the name suggests, they are characterized by having five pairs of legs (deca= ten; poda= feet), with three of the eight thoracic appendages having become integrated into the head to function as mouthparts. The taxonomic divisions within the Decapoda are not as clear and there is still much to be learned about the relationships of the different groups. The **Brachyura** (pg. 13) are considered the "true crabs"; the first pair of legs are claws while the remaining four pairs serve as walking legs. Many **Anomura** (pg. 57) superficially resemble the true crabs but appear to have only three pairs of walking legs following

2

their claws. In this group the last fifth pair of legs are often greatly reduced in size and kept folded in the gill chamber, and the tiny claws and brushes on the tip are used to clean the gills and other parts of the body. They can also be distinguished from the Brachyura by the placement of the second antennae, which appear lateral or outside of the eyes instead of between the eyes.

The term 'shrimp' is commonly used for a number of distantly-related groups. The burrowing or ghost shrimps (**Thalassinidea**, pg. 78) were long classified as anomurans but may be more closely allied with the lobsters. These typically have reduced eyes and a fairly soft, thin exoskeleton, and tend to remain underground. Only a few **Penaeoidea** (pg. 79) occur within diving depths along our Pacific coast, but in the tropics they are an abundant and diverse group of tremendous economic importance. Penaeids have a gill structure unique among decapods and also differ in reproduction, being the only ones to freely spawn their eggs instead of brooding them.

Nearly all of the shrimps in our area belong to the **Caridea** (pg. 35), but, despite their strong resemblance to the penaeids, they are probably more closely related to crabs. At first glance there would seem to be little in common between a crab and a shrimp, but their body plans are actually quite similar. A crab is essentially a shrimp with its abdomen reduced in size and folded tightly beneath the body, and if you straighten out the abdomen of a crab this becomes more apparent (Fig. 1). The large, muscular abdomen of a shrimp is used for swimming quickly backwards to escape predators, while paired appendages called pleopods are used both to swim forward and also for brooding the eggs. Brachyuran crabs have lost all ability to swim with their abdomens and for the most part have also lost the appendages; the last pair (uropods) that form much of the tail fan used in backward swimming by shrimps and lobsters is missing entirely. The pleopods are retained only for egg brooding in female crabs, and in males reduced to just two pairs that are used in copulation.

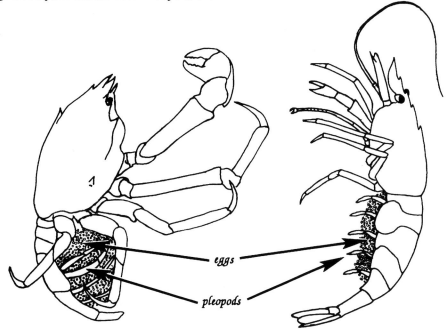

eggs

pleopods

Figure 1

Growth

Every summer the bodies of countless Dungeness crabs begin littering coastal beaches, prompting concerns about the health of crab stocks. While true that diseases can decimate crustacean populations, more often than not closer examination of these "corpses" reveals that they have no meat in them and are merely the cast off exoskeletons from live crabs. One of the disadvantages of being protected by a hard shell is the constraint it places on growth, for in order to increase in size an arthropod must periodically molt or shed its "skin". The act of molting is a dramatic event and results in a sudden large increase in size, but this growth is more apparent than real. Growth in terms of actual weight gain and muscle mass occurs during the period between molts, and for this reason a soft crab that has just molted to legal size contains only a little bit of watery meat because it has no more muscle than it did at its smaller size.

Molting is a remarkable process. A molting crab leaves behind an exact (and usually intact) replicate of itself, down to the surface of its eyes and gills and even the lining of its stomach and hindgut. The animal backs out through a split along the rear edge of the carapace where it connects to the abdomen, with the entire process taking from minutes to hours depending on its age, size, and species. While molting *per se* takes relatively little time, one must keep in mind that the entire new exoskeleton had to first be made during the weeks leading up to molting.

Considering how large the claw is in some species and the comparatively minuscule diameter at the base of the limb, it seems inconceivable that so much tissue could be pulled through all at once. In fact, most use some sleight of hand in the process: before molting, as much as 40% of the musculature of the claw may be broken down to be reconstructed later. This material is stored in the digestive gland, and its absence also adds to the apparent "wateriness" of a soft crab. Another trick often used in extracting large claws from the molt involves a special weak spot near the narrow juncture connecting the claw to the body that can pop open and provide a much larger opening for extraction of the claw.

A newly-molted crab has little ability to defend itself and is vulnerable to many more predators than usual. In anticipation of this many seek refuge or seclusion prior to molting, while others may bury in the sediment immediately after molting is completed. Crabs stop feeding shortly before molting and do not resume until they have hardened up somewhat, a process that may take from hours to many days depending on the size of the crab.

Molting has some clear advantages, too. In addition to growth, it affords a crustacean the chance to rid its exoskeleton of unwanted barnacles and other material and to replace missing limbs. Claws and walking legs usually have a pre-formed breakage plane near their base that allows the limb to be dropped off if it is seized by a predator or damaged beyond repair. During the weeks leading up to molting, a nonfunctional limb bud develops on the remaining scar, which then becomes a smaller than normal but usable appendage when the animal molts. The energy required to regenerate several missing limbs can affect overall growth to such an extent that the carapace may even decrease in size. As with most other organisms, the growth rate is fastest in the young and decreases with age; for example, a Dungeness crab may average nearly one molt per month in its first year while an adult only molts once annually. Some stop molting entirely. In spider crabs, the final molt coincides with reaching sexual maturity and there is usually a sudden increase in sexual characteristics such as the size of the male's claws and the width of the abdomen in females. Even in those species that continue to molt and grow, the differences between sexes become more apparent with age, probably because females must invest a considerable amount of energy into egg production while males can devote more towards growth.

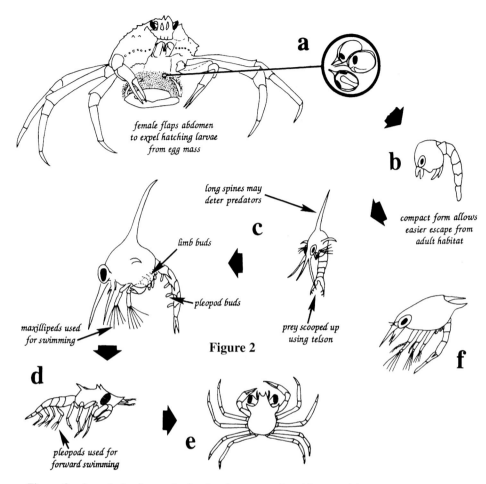

Figure 2. Larval development of a brachyuran crab. (a) eggs; (b) prezoea; (c) zoea; (d) megalops; (e) first juvenile instar; (f) typical zoea of an anomuran crab.

Within the figure:
female flaps abdomen to expel hatching larvae from egg mass

compact form allows easier escape from adult habitat

long spines may deter predators

limb buds

pleopod buds

maxillipeds used for swimming

prey scooped up using telson

Figure 2

pleopods used for forward swimming

Reproduction and Development

Reproduction in decapods is often inextricably linked with the molt cycle because the females of many species are capable of mating only while soft-shelled. This constraint is particularly interesting considering the range of mating techniques and strategies that exist among the different groups; for example, the eggs of shrimps and anomuran crabs are fertilized externally shortly after mating, while brachyuran crabs typically have internal fertilization and females may store sperm for a fairly long time before using it to fertilize their eggs. Competition for mating opportunities has led to the evolution of a fascinating variety of strategies, behaviors, and structural differences. Much like the familiar horns and antlers of terrestrial mammals, the males of many crustaceans develop larger claws than females, in some cases (e.g. fiddler crabs) becoming so exaggerated that they can no longer function as feeding appendages. Enlarged claws are as much for show as fighting since many contests are settled by displays rather than physical conflict; when actual sparring does occur it is usually with closed claws and fights rarely escalate to the point where contestants are injured.

Females approaching molt apparently release a scent or pheromone that signals their receptivity to males and this attraction is so strong in some species that fisherman have used

5

premolt females as "bait" to attract male crabs. When a male encounters a receptive female, he grasps her in a precopulatory embrace that can last from hours to even weeks depending on how close the female is to molting. Female *Cancer* crabs are normally enveloped by the male's claws and carried in a face-to-face position, but when pressured by rivals a male will sometimes transfer her to his last pair of legs to keep his claws free for defense. Some species tend to aggregate during mating season, and having large numbers of females releasing pheromones in an area can cause confusion and may account for occasional cases of misguided affection. During the height of the mating season male Dungeness crabs are sometimes found trying to embrace female (and even male) red rock crabs, and one particularly disoriented male was spotted clutching an empty can of Dr. Pepper®!

When the female molts, the male loosens his grasp and may even assist her in working free of the old exoskeleton before repositioning her for mating. In male brachyuran crabs, the two pairs of pleopods (gonopods) combine to form a sort of syringe that is used to pump sperm into the seminal receptacle, or spermatheca, of the female. The sperm passes from the short penes (located on the base of the last pair of legs) into a groove in the first gonopod, while the second gonopod functions as the piston or plunger in the groove to push the sperm into the female. In some species, the tip of the first gonopod is ornamented with hooks or bristles and it is suspected that they are used to remove the sperm of other males that may already be in the spermatheca. Although not yet proven for crabs, this strategy is well-known in some insects and the structure of some species' gonopods suggests a similar function. Females of some brachyuran crabs can mate while hard-shelled. At certain times the openings of the gonopores become softened, making copulation possible. Hardshell mating tends to be of very short duration and is more common among species that live high in the intertidal and on land. Interestingly, crabs that mate hardshelled copulate with the female on top, while in softshelled matings the male assumes the upper position.

Detailed observations of mating by lithodid crabs are available only for king crab. Male king crab lack gonopods and instead use their reduced fifth pair of legs to smear sperm directly onto the pleopods of the female, so that the eggs are fertilized after they are extruded. Mating in shrimps is a similar but much quicker affair, usually lacking the prolonged embraces and mate guarding. The male shrimp attaches a sperm packet to the underside of the female, and when the female extrudes her eggs she uses her legs to scratch open the packet and release the sperm.

Following mating, the male crab usually continues to embrace the female, probably helping to protect her from predators during this vulnerable period and also preventing other males from getting access to the female. Some species take this a step further by plugging the genital openings of the female with a hard substance which may serve as a "chastity belt" to prevent rivals from mating with that female.

With the exception of the penaeid shrimps, all decapods brood their eggs on their pleopods. The female meticulously cares for the eggs, picking out the dead ones and periodically shaking the egg mass to aerate them. Development times vary from several weeks to a year or more and there is generally a correlation between egg size and development time, with larger eggs taking longer to hatch. The biggest eggs are usually those from species in very deep water and hatch into large, nonfeeding larvae. Reproduction occurs year-round under the relatively constant conditions at these depths. In contrast, the larvae of most shallow-water decapods feed on smaller planktonic organisms and have their reproduction timed so that larvae can take advantage of the spring and summer plankton blooms. When eggs are ready to hatch, the female crab typically elevates herself on the tips of her walking legs and lowers her abdomen to expose the eggs, releasing pulses of larvae with hard shakes of her abdomen and pleopods (Fig. 2a). In some species, this behavior is initiated by a chemical cue given off by the eggs that signals their readiness to hatch.

Decapods usually hatch in a form called the prezoea (Fig. 2b). This is not a true larval stage but rather a very compact form that is still partially enclosed by egg membrane, and probably reduces the chance of getting carapace spines entangled in algae or other debris in the adult habitat. This final membrane is usually shed within minutes of hatching and the zoea's spines expand and harden, no doubt making it much more difficult for a small predator to swallow. Zoeae swim using their maxillipeds and at this stage the biramous form of these mouthparts is clearly visible, the long hairs on the tips of the exopods making propulsion possible. Feeding is accomplished using the flattened, spiny end of the abdomen to scoop up smaller plants and animals and press them to the mouth.

Over the course of succeeding molts, the zoeae develop limb buds that are the precursors of the claws and walking legs; in the last zoeal stage, pleopod buds appear. The number and duration of zoeal stages varies considerably among the different groups but tend to be somewhat consistent at the family level. The Majidae or spider crabs have only two zoeal stages, while Cancer crabs (Cancridae) have five; the Lithodidae (king crabs) typically have four zoeae. One notable exception are shrimps of the family Crangonidae, which run the gamut from five or more zoeae that feed (*Crangon*) to two very brief, nonfeeding zoeal stages (*Paracrangon*) to none whatsoever (*Sclerocrangon*), essentially hatching as a juvenile shrimp.

After spending weeks or months drifting as zoeae in the plankton the decapod larvae molt to a stage known as the megalops (Fig. 2d). Crab megalopae look much like a cross between a crab and a shrimp: the claws, legs, and carapace are distinctly crablike but the abdomen extends fully and is equipped with a full set of pleopods for swimming. Because it can both swim and crawl, this stage is ideally suited for its sole function of finding the proper juvenile habitat in which to settle out. Megalopae of some *Cancer* crabs are often found hitching rides on jellyfish, possibly using this relatively safe (and edible) transportation to get to nearshore areas. Very little is known about how this stage reaches and recognizes the right area, but recent work with porcelain crabs has shown that their megalopae select the proper habitat by sensing odors from adults of their own species, and actually gain protection from predators by settling underneath them.

The larvae of decapod crustaceans bear so little resemblance to their parents that they were once classified as entirely different organisms: *Zoea* and *Megalops* were in fact genera until it was demonstrated that they were the young stages of crabs. Identification of larval decapods to species is still often difficult, and the task even more daunting considering that many Pacific coast species have never been described. Given a reasonable amount of care and minimal investment in materials, the larvae of many species can be easily reared in captivity to provide a series for descriptions. This is just one area of research where the dedicated amateur can make important and lasting contributions.

How to use this book:

The illustrated key (pg. 9) can be used to determine the families of west coast decapods and from there the photographs can be used to determine the species. Each photograph is accompanied by the following information:

Identification: This section emphasizes characters that help to distinguish it from similar species, along with notes on color variations. *Size*: Maximum recorded size given as carapace width for crabs, carapace length for hermit crabs, and total body length (tip of rostrum to end of telson) for shrimp (Fig. 3). *Range*: Recorded extent of distribution. Whenever possible, I have tried to indicate areas of greatest abundance. *Habitat*: Type of area where a species is normally found, along with the depths at which it is known to occur. As with ranges, depth records often greatly exceed the normal distribution of the species and typical depths are given, if known. *Remarks*: Additional information on feeding habits, behavior, symbiotic associations, similar species that are not pictured, and other notes of interest. The often meager pickings of this section highlight just how little is known about the ecology of many of the species on our coast.

An asterisk (*) denotes information from my own research that has not been previously published, while the reference section lists sources of information used in compiling the species profiles. The common names used are (for the most part) those recommended by the American Fisheries Society, except in those cases where a preexisting name was already well-entrenched in popular publications or the diving community. In a few cases I have omitted the recommended name because it is either inappropriate or unacceptably long and unwieldy, but in most cases those without names have just never been given one.

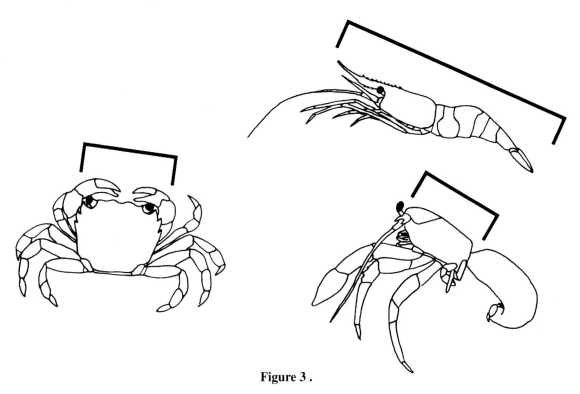

Figure 3 .

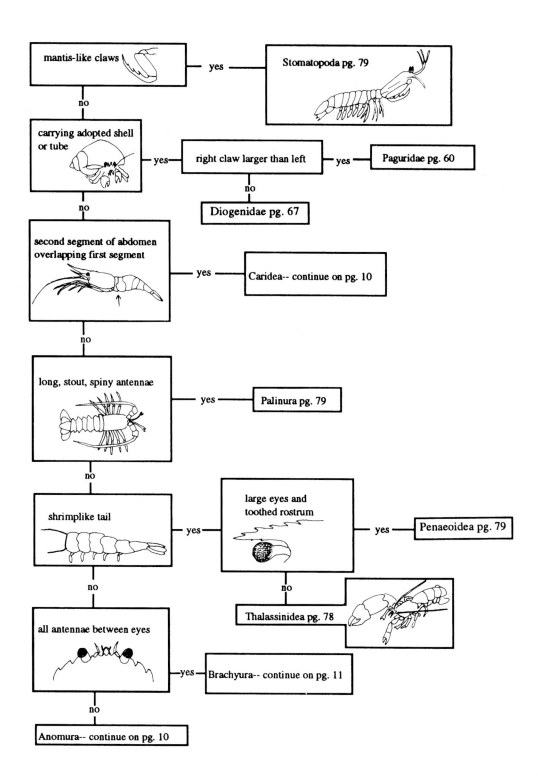

mantis-like claws → yes → Stomatopoda pg. 79

no

carrying adopted shell or tube → yes → right claw larger than left → yes → Paguridae pg. 60

no → Diogenidae pg. 67

no

second segment of abdomen overlapping first segment → yes → Caridea-- continue on pg. 10

no

long, stout, spiny antennae → yes → Palinura pg. 79

no

shrimplike tail → yes → large eyes and toothed rostrum → yes → Penaeoidea pg. 79

no → Thalassinidea pg. 78

no

all antennae between eyes → yes → Brachyura-- continue on pg. 11

no

Anomura-- continue on pg. 10

CARIDEA

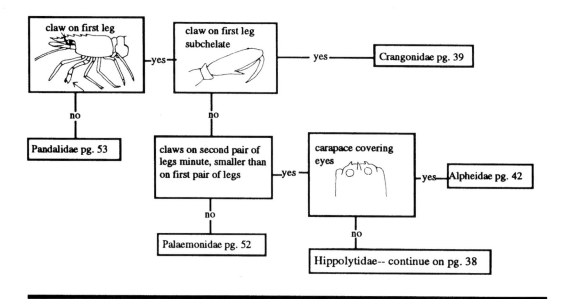

claw on first leg
—yes—
claw on first leg subchelate
—yes——— Crangonidae pg. 39

no
Pandalidae pg. 53

no
claws on second pair of legs minute, smaller than on first pair of legs
—yes—
carapace covering eyes
—yes— Alpheidae pg. 42

no
Palaemonidae pg. 52

no
Hippolytidae-- continue on pg. 38

ANOMURA

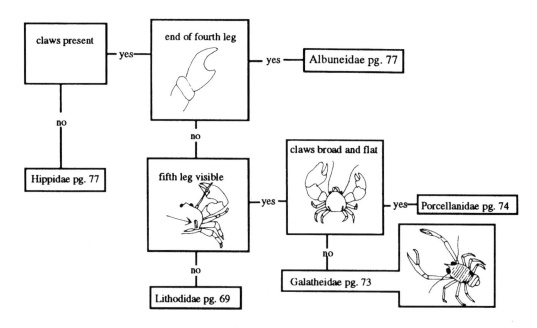

claws present
—yes—
end of fourth leg
—yes— Albuneidae pg. 77

no
Hippidae pg. 77

no
fifth leg visible
—yes—
claws broad and flat
—yes— Porcellanidae pg. 74

no
Galatheidae pg. 73

no
Lithodidae pg. 69

BRACHYURA

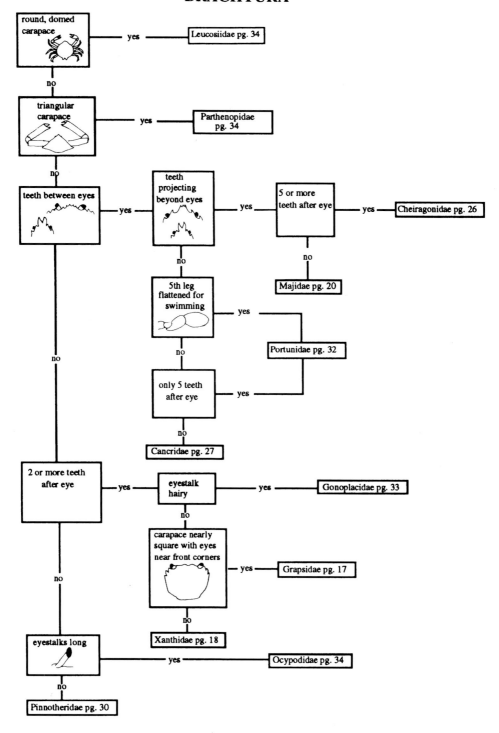

round, domed carapace — yes → Leucosiidae pg. 34

no

triangular carapace — yes → Parthenopidae pg. 34

no

teeth between eyes — yes → teeth projecting beyond eyes — yes → 5 or more teeth after eye — yes → Cheiragonidae pg. 26

no (from 5 or more teeth after eye) → Majidae pg. 20

no (from teeth projecting beyond eyes) → 5th leg flattened for swimming — yes → Portunidae pg. 32

no → only 5 teeth after eye — yes → Portunidae pg. 32

no → Cancridae pg. 27

no (from teeth between eyes) → 2 or more teeth after eye — yes → eyestalk hairy — yes → Gonoplacidae pg. 33

no → carapace nearly square with eyes near front corners — yes → Grapsidae pg. 17

no → Xanthidae pg. 18

no (from 2 or more teeth after eye) → eyestalks long — yes → Ocypodidae pg. 34

no → Pinnotheridae pg. 30

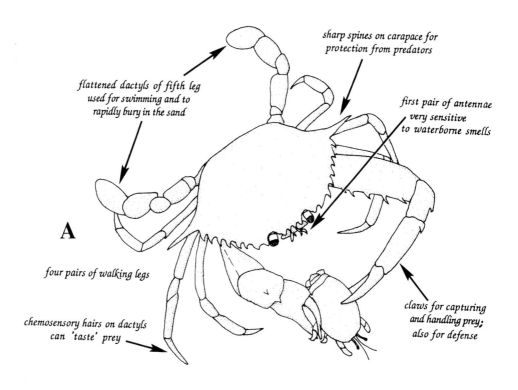

A

sharp spines on carapace for
protection from predators

flattened dactyls of fifth leg
used for swimming and to
rapidly bury in the sand

first pair of antennae
very sensitive
to waterborne smells

four pairs of walking legs

claws for capturing
and handling prey;
also for defense

chemosensory hairs on dactyls
can 'taste' prey

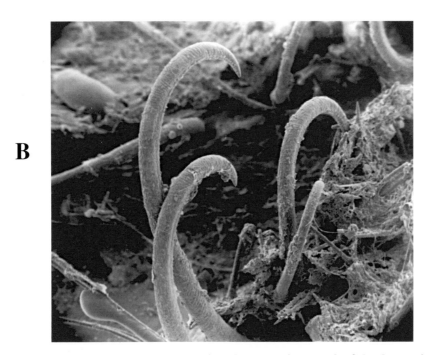

B

Figure 4. (a) swimming crab; (b) scanning electron micrograph of the decorating setae of
Hyas lyratus.

Brachyura

The decapod body attains its most compact form in the Brachyura or "true" crabs (Fig. 4a). Here the third maxillipeds have been fully integrated into the head to form door-like coverings for the mouthparts and the second pair of antennae have become greatly reduced. The abdomen is not used in locomotion and its appendages retained only for reproduction; in some cases abdominal segments have even become partly fused. Brachyurans lack a specialized gill cleaning appendage equivalent to the second leg of shrimps or the fifth leg of anomurans. Instead, they have feather-like extensions arising from the base of each maxilliped that reach far back into the gill chamber and sweep over the surface of the gills whenever the mouthparts are moved.

The **Grapsidae** (pg. 17) are familiar to anyone who has turned over rocks at the seashore. Shore crabs typically have a squarish carapace and fairly large eyes, and are considerably faster and more agile out of water than most other crabs. All three of the common Pacific coast species live fairly high in the intertidal zone and can be found in a surprisingly wide range of habitats and substrates. In addition to preying opportunistically on smaller animals and scavenging, they use the spoon-like tips of their claws to scrape diatoms and algae off the surface of rocks.

Some of the **Xanthidae** (pg. 18) superficially resemble the shore crabs but a closer examination will reveal differences both in their appearance and especially their behavior. These slow moving crabs often completely stiffen their claws and legs when picked up, but can suddenly snap out of this "rigor mortis" and deliver a painful pinch if carelessly handled. Most local species are omnivorous, feeding on algae and sessile organisms such as barnacles and small bivalves. They are usually found partially buried in the sediment beneath large rocks.

Named for their long, spindly legs, the distinctive spider crabs (**Majidae**, pg. 20) are perhaps best known for their habit of camouflaging themselves using bits of algae, sponges, bryozoans, or other material. This behavior probably began as a means of storing extra food and some (e.g. *Podochela*) still use it that way. Others have become adapted to open mud or sand bottoms and appear to have lost this behavior, but most continue to decorate themselves at least partially, especially when they are juveniles. A few do their job thoroughly, fastidiously attaching material over their entire carapace and along each of their legs, while others may only place a single sprig of algae on their rostrum or appear to let their roughened carapaces passively collect fouling organisms. The fragments are attached to special patches of small, stiff, curved hairs (Fig. 4b), and over time may become attached and grow. In addition to making the crab hard to see, it also changes the way it feels, smells, and tastes to a predator, and the materials themselves may be noxious. Decorators lose their handiwork when they shed their exoskeleton just as other crabs rid themselves of unwanted barnacles, but many recoup their losses by salvaging what they can from their old shell shortly after molting.

Spider crabs are not particularly fast or graceful and usually rely on cryptic coloration or their decorations for protection. When this fails, many extend their elongate first walking leg to ward off intruders, while northern kelp crabs (*Pugettia producta*) are often very aggressive and sometimes hurl themselves onto unsuspecting divers. *Pugettia* is one of the few large organisms that grazes directly on large kelp, but in the winter, when the beds disappear, their diet shifts to barnacles and the occasional passing jellyfish that strays too close (Fig. 5). The different species of spider crabs can often be recognized by their carapace outlines alone (Fig. 6).

The family **Cancridae** (pg. 27) includes one of the more familiar and commercially important crustaceans on our coast, the Dungeness crab, *Cancer magister*, along with several other species of sport or commercial value. This family is confined to cold and temperate waters and is easily recognized by the many teeth along the edges of the carapace following the eyes. All of them are predators and most feed primarily on bivalves such as clams and mussels. Because they respond to baited traps, they are often assumed to be scavengers, when in fact they are just being opportunistic and taking advantage what appears to be a free meal. These large crabs may have a much greater effect on benthic communities than merely playing a role in the food chain as predators on smaller organisms and prey for large fish and octopus. I have observed them excavating large horseclams (*Tresus* spp.) while hoards of small bottomfish waited to share in the feast, and when crabs consumed their hard-won prizes, the fish moved with impunity between and beneath their claws and legs to steal bits of meat. By uncovering and opening such inaccessible prey, the crabs may function as a conduit for resources that would normally remain unavailable, and considering the number of pock marks left behind from their diggings, this could provide a substantial contribution to the diet of fish in some areas.

A frequent casualty of such excavations are the pea crabs (**Pinnotheridae**, pg. 30) inhabiting the mantle cavities of the clams. The members of this group are small, often soft-bodied crabs that typically live in association with larger invertebrates. The common species found inside clams and mussels are familiar to most clam diggers, but there are many other, more cryptic species that inhabit tunicates and the tubes and burrows made by worms and thalassinid shrimps. Though most appear to have little effect on their host, the activities of those inside bivalves do result in some damage to the clam's gills. Within the area covered by this book, there are at least 14 species within the genus *Pinnixa* alone, and many are difficult to identify. Only a few of the more common and distinctive species have been included here; for others the reader should consult the keys in Hart (1982) and Zmarzly (1992).

The swimming crabs or **Portunidae** (pg. 32) are an important and diverse family in tropical waters. Only a few occur far enough north to make it up into southern California, but recently the number of species has been nearly doubled due to introductions from the east coast of the green crab, *Carcinus maenas*, and the blue crab, *Callinectes sapidus*. Portunids are usually lightly built and quick and most are superb swimmers that have flattened dactyls on their last pair of legs for propelling themselves. They prey on a wide variety of smaller organisms and are often agile and fast enough to catch fish and shrimp.

The **Cheiragonidae** (pg. 26) is a small family confined to the north Pacific, with two species occurring along the northern part of our coast. These odd, bristly crabs are large enough to attract some interest as food, and at least one species, the hair crab, *Erimacrus isenbeckii*, has been exported to Asian markets.

A few other families that are primarily tropical have just single representatives venturing into the southern part of our area. Small, remnant populations are all that is left of the only species of fiddler crab (**Ocypodidae**; pg. 34) occurring in southern California. This large and distinctive family is widespread in tropical and subtropical waters, typically burrowing in the high intertidal mud of salt marshes and mangrove swamps. Unfortunately, our lone fiddler has suffered badly at the hands of shoreline developers, with much of its habitat having been destroyed in the name of such "improvements" as marinas and condominiums. Our only example of the **Gonoplacidae**, *Malacoplax* (formerly *Speocarcinus*) *californiensis* (pg. 33), constructs burrows in the mud of bays and estuaries along with the fiddler crab and appears to have fared even worse than its neighbor, though it is unlikely that its decline is solely due to habitat loss. Early copies of "Between Pacific Tides" described it as ubiquitous throughout Newport Bay, while later editions noted that it had since become rare; it is now difficult to find anyone who has ever seen a living specimen.

The tropical family **Leucosiidae** also has but one representative, the odd-looking globose sand crab, *Randallia ornata* (pg. 34). Many members of this family have beautiful carapace markings and a highly polished surface that combine to give one the impression of a cowry shell. Even more bizarre are the **Parthenopidae** (pg. 34), with their extremely elongate claws that end in absurdly small pincers. Observations of captive specimens suggest that these seemingly ineffectual limbs are very efficient tools, with the entire appendage being used like a clamp to seize prey between the long opposing faces of the merus and propodus. In addition, the pincer can be used like a pipe wrench to pry apart barnacles and other hardshelled prey, with the long "elbows" providing leverage.

Figure 5. Northern kelp crabs (*Pugettia producta*) consuming a large jellyfish that drifted too close to their piling.

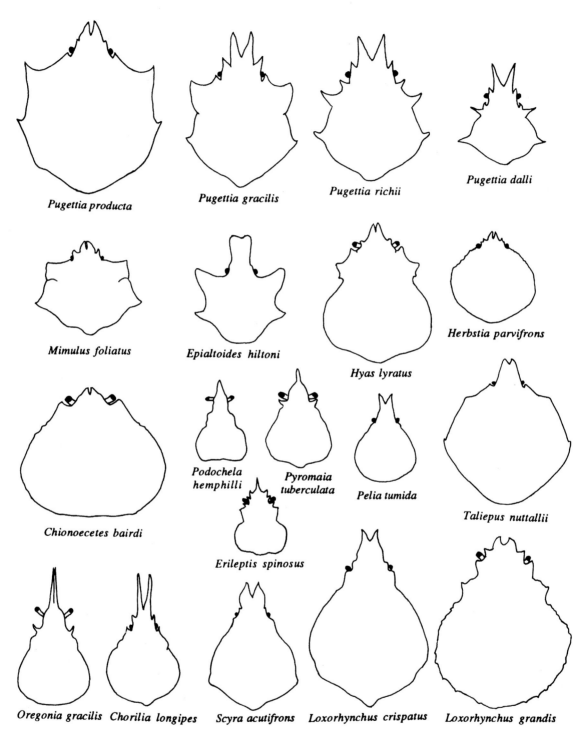

Figure 6. Carapace outlines of Pacific coast spider crabs (Family Majidae).

Family GRAPSIDAE

1. *Hemigrapsus nudus*

Purple shore crab

Identification: Carapace with three teeth following eye; walking legs not hairy. Adults normally dark purple, but olive green or reddish-brown specimens are not uncommon. Claws with distinctive reddish spots and white tips; . Juveniles variable in color and pattern. *Size*: Males to 56 mm (2.2 in); females 34 mm (1.3 in). *Range*: Yakobi Island, Alaska to Bahia de Tortuga, Mexico; uncommon in southern California. *Habitat*: Under rocks in the high and middle intertidal of exposed beaches; also in some estuaries. *Remarks*: Forages along the tops of rocks during nighttime low tides and will also venture out onto nearby sand beaches.

2. *Hemigrapsus oregonensis*

Yellow shore crab

Identification: Distinguished from *H. nudus* [1] by its hairy legs and the lack of reddish spots on the claws. Color usually a dark or grayish green, but white or mottled patterns are common, especially among juveniles. *Size*: To 49.5 mm (1.9 in). *Range*: Resurrection Bay, Alaska to Baja California. *Habitat*: Found under rocks throughout the intertidal zone, especially on muddy or gravelly beaches, and in estuaries where it constructs burrows in mud banks. Generally prefers more protected, quiet water areas than *H. nudus* but the two species often occur together. *Remarks:* Easily the most abundant and widespread crab in the Puget Sound region and San Francisco Bay. In addition to scraping up diatoms and cropping algae, it also preys on a wide range of smaller invertebrates, scavenges whenever possible, and can even filter-feed* using its third maxillipeds.

3. *Pachygrapsus crassipes*

Striped shore crab

Identification: Distinguished from *Hemigrapsus* by its striped markings, carapace with only two teeth following the eye, and toothed expansion on the end of the merus of the claw. *Size*: To 48 mm (1.9 in). *Range*: Ecola State Park, Oregon* to Gulf of California; also introduced to Japan in the late nineteenth century. *Habitat*: Upper and middle intertidal of rocky beaches; also found in some estuaries where it appropriates and enlarges *H. oregonensis* [2] burrows after eating the occupant. *Remarks*: Forages both in and out of water and is quite active during the daytime, where it can be seen moving about on the tops and sides of rocks. More inclined to pinch when handled than either species of *Hemigrapsus* and much quicker, and has even been reported to catch flies at low tide.

17

Family XANTHIDAE

4. *Pilumnus spinohirsutus*
Retiring southerner

Identification: Carapace, claws, and legs adorned with a stiff covering of light brown hair that obscures the five sharp, curved spines along the edge of the carapace. Claws with dark fingers. *Size*: To 35 mm (1.3 in). *Range*: San Pedro, California to Baja California. *Habitat*: Usually well-concealed in sand beneath and between rocks, in protected and semi-protected areas. Found from the low intertidal to 25 m (80 ft). *Remarks*: Abundant among clusters of tube mollusks (*Serpulorbus squamigerus*). Captive specimens are strictly carnivorous.

5. *Rhithropanopeus harrisii*
Brackish-water crab

Identification: Strongly resembles the green shore crab *Hemigrapsus oregonensis* [2] both in color and shape, but can be distinguished by its more rounded outline and the dorsal ridges on the front half of the carapace. Color a dull green, with white-tipped, unequal claws. *Size*: Males to 19 mm (0.75 in); females 10.6 mm (0.4 in). *Range*: An Atlantic species that was first reported from San Francisco Bay in 1940 and has since spread to Coos Bay, Oregon. *Habitat*: Limited to estuaries, where it lives under rocks in brackish water and can also venture up into fresh water. *Remarks*: Abundant in some areas of San Francisco Bay, where it can be found under rocks with the faster moving *Hemigrapsus oregonensis*.

6. *Cycloxanthops novemdentatus*
Pebble crab

Identification: Carapace oval in outline and with nine small, somewhat indistinct teeth following eye. Color varies from brown to orange or purple; claws with black fingers. *Size*: Males to 100 mm (3.9 in); females 52 mm (2 in). *Range*: Monterey Bay to Punta Abreojos, Baja California. *Habitat*: Low intertidal to 73 m (240 ft). Occurs in sandier areas than other Pacific coast xanthids, excavating cavities beneath boulders that rest on coarse sand. Juveniles tend to be found at slightly higher tidal levels, among gravel or shell in rocky areas. *Remarks*: Easily mistaken for a small *Cancer* crab but lacks the five teeth between the eyes. It is primarily active at night, when it emerges from hiding to feed on algae, worms, crustaceans, and sea urchins. Unusually fast and aggressive compared to other Pacific coast xanthids, whom it readily preys upon.

18

7. *Lophopanopeus bellus*
Black-clawed crab

Identification: Carapace broadest anteriorly, with three teeth on each side; walking legs with small hairs on the carpus and propodus. Color and pattern extremely variable, ranging from purple and orange to brown, white, or mottled; fingers of claws almost always very dark. *Size*: Males to 40.5 mm* (1.6 in); females 24 mm (0.9 in). *Range*: Resurrection Bay, Alaska to Point Sur, California. *Habitat*: Found partially buried in sand or gravel under rocks in the low intertidal zone, and often in discarded bottles subtidally. To 80 m (260 ft). *Remarks*: Omnivorous, feeding on algae, small mollusks, and barnacles. Specimens often display "rigor mortis" type behavior when handled. Two subspecies are known: *L. bellus bellus* (pictured), and *L. bellus diegensis*. The latter has pronounced lobes on its walking legs and tubercles on the carpus of the claw, and has been found from Prince William Sound, Alaska to San Diego. It is strictly subtidal in the northern part of its range but reported from intertidal areas in southern California.

8. *Lophopanopeus frontalis*

Identification: Can be distinguished from other west coast *Lophopanopeus* by its claws, which lack the usual large molar at the base of the movable finger and almost always have the dark color of the fixed finger conspicuously extending back onto the hand. *Size*: Males to 24 mm (0.9 in); females 13 mm (0.5 in). *Range*: Santa Monica Bay, California to Bahia Magdalena, Baja California. *Habitat*: Found from the low intertidal to 37 m (120 ft). Occurs under rocks in bays and is also reported from clusters of mussels on pilings. *Remarks*: Captive specimens were primarily herbivorous.

9. *Paraxanthias taylori*
Lumpy crab

Identification: Easily distinguished by the prominent bumps covering the surface of the claws. Walking legs very hairy. Color typically a very polished-looking reddish-brown; claws with reddish or brown fingers. Size: Male carapace width to 25 mm (1 in); females 42 mm (1.6 in). *Range*: Monterey to Baja California. *Habitat*: Middle intertidal to 100 m (328 ft). Found under rocks, sometimes partially buried in sand, and in kelp holdfasts. *Remarks*: This shy crab feeds mainly on red and green algae.

10. *Lophopanopeus leucomanus*

Identification: Virtually identical to the black-clawed crab *L. bellus,* but lacking hair on the carpus and propodus of the walking legs. Highly variable in color and pattern; often tan, brown, or orange. *Size*: Males 21 mm (0.8 in); females 17 mm (0.6 in). *Range*: Carmel, California to Rosarito, Baja California. *Habitat*: Found intertidally on protected or semi-protected beaches, buried under rocks in coarse sand and to a depth of 200 m (656 ft). *Remarks*: Feeds on encrusting algae and smaller invertebrates. Divided into two subspecies: *L. l. leucomanus* (pictured) with irregular pits and ridges on the carpus of the claw and lobes on the carpus of the walking legs, and the southern form *L.l.heathii* with a smooth carpus (found from Moss Beach to La Jolla).

Family MAJIDAE

11. *Chionoecetes bairdi*
Tanner crab

Identification: Carapace slightly wider than long and with a very short, flattened rostrum. Claws much shorter than walking legs and with slender, curved fingers. Color light brown or greenish brown, with irridescent sheen on claws; eyes with reddish corneas. *Size*: Males to 140 mm (5.5 in); females to 81 mm (3.2 in). *Range*: Bering Sea to Winchester Bay, Oregon. *Habitat*: Found on open mud or sand bottoms, from 6-474 m (20-1555 ft). Usually only juveniles are found within normal diving depths in Washington. *Remarks*: An important commercial species in Alaskan waters, where it is fished with pots and marketed as snow crab. It preys on a wide range of organisms including small clams and crabs, especially juveniles of its own species.

12. *Hyas lyratus*
Pacific lyre crab
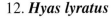

Identification: Named for its lyre-shaped carapace, with prominent expansions immediately following eye and no teeth on the remainder of the carapace. Carapace usually grayish or tan; tends to carry few or no decorations. *Size*: Males to 80 mm (3.1 in); females 46 mm (1.8 in). *Range*: Bering Sea to Puget Sound, Washington. *Habitat*: Typically found on mixed-composition bottoms at depths of 9-640 m (30-2000 ft) often with *Oregonia gracilis* [20]. *Remarks*: Researchers in Alaska recently discovered large breeding aggregations of lyre crabs on flat silt-mud bottoms in deep water, forming mounds a foot high and composed of approximately 2000 crabs.

13. *Scyra acutifrons*

Sharpnose crab

Identification: Rostrum composed of two flattened, leaflike horns with rounded outside edges; surface of carapace very irregular. Adult males (pictured) with exceptionally large, long claws; walking legs relatively short and stout. The brownish or tan carapace is often obscured by sponges and bryozoans, but orange markings on the claws are usually visible. *Size*: To 45 mm (1.7 in). *Range*: Kodiak, Alaska to Punta San Carlos, Mexico; uncommon south of Pacific Grove, California. *Habitat*: Most abundant subtidally on the large boulders of breakwaters and similar rocky situations, usually among dense coverings of invertebrates rather than around algae. Reported from the low intertidal to 220 m (720 ft). *Remarks*: This species puts relatively little effort into decorating, occasionally placing a small piece of material on its rostrum but generally appearing to just let organisms colonize its roughened carapace. It feeds primarily on detritus and sessile invertebrates, and sometimes associates with sea anemones.

14. *Herbstia parvifrons*

Crevice spider crab

Identification: A very distinctive and atypical spider crab, having a carapace that is almost circular in outline except for the rostrum. Walking legs with very spiny margins. Color tan to orange, with faint banding on walking legs. *Size*: Males to 41 mm (1.6 in); females 17 mm (0.6 in). *Range*: Monterey, California to Baja California. *Habitat*: Under rocks and in crevices, from the low intertidal to 73 m (240 ft). Most commonly found in shallow subtidal areas where fairly large rocks rest on other rocks. *Remarks*: Unlike other spider crabs, this species moves quickly and retreats into crevices for protection. It is often overgrown with a small, white, fingerlike sponge.

15. *Pugettia gracilis*

Graceful kelp crab

Identification: Margin of carapace indented between the large lateral teeth; surface fairly smooth with a few bumps but no spines. Rostral horns large, divergent. Fingers of claws grayish or blue, with orange tips. Carapace color highly variable (especially in young specimens), ranging from white to bright red. Size: Carapace width to 34 mm (1.3 in). *Range*: Aleutian Islands to Monterey. *Habitat*: Found among rocks and algae both on the outer coast and in protected inshore waters, where juveniles are often very common in eelgrass beds. Low intertidal to 140 m (460 ft). *Remarks*: Puts very little effort into decorating, usually wearing little more than a piece of algae on its rostrum.

16. *Pugettia producta*

Northern kelp crab

Identification: Carapace broad and smooth with margin of carapace between lateral teeth straight; rostrum relatively short . Color kelp brown or dark red; underside yellow or scarlet. Juveniles either red or olive green. *Size*: Males to 93 mm (3.6 in); females 78 mm (3 in). *Range*: Prince of Wales Island, Alaska to Baja California. *Habitat*: Adults are abundant in the kelp canopy and also common on wharf pilings, while juveniles are found intertidally among algae and under rocks. Recorded to 73 m (240 ft). *Remarks*: Although small specimens often have a single piece of algae attached to their rostrums, adults are typically devoid of such intentional decorations and rely on their coloration and feisty disposition for protection. Large, old shell crabs living on pilings are often covered with barnacles. An important prey item for sea otters in California.

17. *Pugettia richii*

Cryptic kelp crab

Identification: Often confused with *P. gracilis* [15], but can be distinguished by the following characters: The lateral carapace teeth are more curved and project at sharper angles; the surface of the carapace has spines; the merus of the claw lacks a dorsal ridge, and the fingers of the claws are white instead of orange and blue. Color ranges from dark brown to scarlet, with more variation apparent in the southern part of the range. *Size*: Males to 42 mm (1.6 in); females 33 mm (1.3 in). *Range*: Prince of Wales Island, Alaska to Baja California. *Habitat*: Limited to areas on or near the outer coast, from the low intertidal to 97 m (318 ft). Usually associated with the giant kelp *Macrocystis*. *Remarks*: Diet consists largely of kelp. Like most other members of this genus, it tends to only decorate the rostrum.

18. *Pugettia dalli*

Spined kelp crab

Identification: A tiny kelp crab having much narrower and more laterally directed carapace teeth than the other species of *Pugettia*, and the only one with club-shaped hairs on the walking legs. Rostrum strongly divergent. Color variable, ranging from dark brown or red to pale green. *Size*: Carapace width to 13.8 mm (0.5 in). *Range*: San Miguel Island, California to Baja California. *Habitat*: Found among algal holdfasts, on docks and pilings, and among surfgrass; intertidal to 117 m (380 ft). *Remarks*: Common but easily overlooked because of its size and heavy decorations. As is typical of spider crabs, sexually mature males have exceptionally large claws compared to females.

19. *Chorilia longipes*

Longhorn decorator crab

Identification: Surface of carapace spiny; rostrum with long, divergent horns. Walking legs slender and lacking hairs. Color predominantly pale orange; often undecorated or decorated with sponges or bryozoans. *Size*: To 45 mm (1.8 in). *Range*: Kodiak, Alaska to Mexico. *Habitat*: Found as shallow as 9 m* (30 ft) to 1190 m (3900 ft). Usually on sand, mud, or shell in deep water, and on boulders or vertical rock faces when found within diving depths. Restricted to deep water in California. *Remarks*: Often mistaken for the more common graceful decorator crab *Oregonia gracilis* [20] which has numerous curved hairs along its walking legs and lacks spines on the carapace.

20. *Oregonia gracilis*

Graceful decorator crab

Identification: Rostral horns long (especially in males) and parallel; carapace largely devoid of spines except for a large curved spine following each eye. Walking legs very long and slender; claws, legs, and carapace covered with hooked setae. Typically grayish or tan, never brightly colored. *Size*: To 39 mm (1.5 in). *Range*: Bering Sea to Monterey; also Japan. *Habitat*: Intertidal and subtidal to 436 m (1430 ft); most abundant in shallow water on mixed composition bottoms. *Remarks*: This is unquestionably the most thorough of all the northern decorators, only equalled in decorating ability in the southern part of its range where its distribution overlaps that of the moss crab, *Loxorhynchus crispatus* [22].

21. *Pelia tumida*

Dwarf teardrop crab

Identification: A tiny crab with a smooth, pear-shaped carapace that is covered with short hairs. The walking legs characteristically appear very thick due to sponges and other material adhering to the stiff hairs along their margins. Males have bright red claws. *Size*: To 14.5 mm (0.5 in) in width. *Range*: Monterey to Bahia de Petatlan, Mexico. *Habitat*: Found under rocks and in kelp holdfasts, from the low intertidal to 100 m (328 ft). *Remarks*: The sponges covering this small crab probably make it distasteful or unrecognizeable to many predators. When disturbed it hunkers down and tightly grips the substrate with the strongly hooked tips of its walking legs.

23

22. *Loxorhynchus crispatus*

Moss crab

Identification: The second largest spider crab in California waters, exceeded in size only by the sheep crab *L. grandis* [23]. Carapace somewhat triangular in outline with a few large, blunt tubercles. Juveniles can be distinguished from the much smaller sharpnose crab *Scyra* [13] by their general hairiness and the shape of their rostral horns, which lack the rounded outside edges typical of *Scyra*. Mature females and juveniles covered with long hairs. *Size*: Males to 123 mm (4.8 in); females 79 mm (3.1 in). *Range*: Humboldt County, California to Isla Natividad, Baja California. *Habitat*: Found among algae and sessile invertebrates from the low intertidal to 183 m (600 ft). *Remarks*: Decorates heavily with algae, bryozoans, sponges, and other invertebrates. Male crabs stop decorating at sexual maturity, by which time they are so large that they have few predators. Diet includes less algae and a considerably wider range of invertebrates than that of most other decorator crabs.

23. *Loxorhynchus grandis*

Sheep crab

Identification: Carapace oval and inflated-looking, with a covering of spines and tubercles; rostrum short and curving distinctly downward. Color a dull gray with some blue on the tubercles and usually masked by decorations in younger specimens. *Size*: Males to 159 mm (6.2 in) in width and females 115 mm (4.5 in), but there are old records of specimens to 273 mm (10.7 in). *Range*: Marin County, California to Punta San Bartolome, Baja California. *Habitat*: Found in rocky areas, although adults often venture out onto open sandy bottoms. Occurs from the low intertidal to 124 m (407 ft). *Remarks*: Like the moss crab *L. crispatus* [22], this species loses the habit of decorating itself when it reaches a large size.

24. *Taliepus nuttallii*

Southern kelp crab

Identification: Carapace very rounded in outline with lateral teeth reduced to small bumps and surface smooth and undecorated; rostral horns fused for most of their length. Juveniles match the color of the kelp, while adults are reddish-brown to bright red. *Size*: Males to 92 mm (3.6 in); females 45 mm (1.8 in). *Range*: Santa Barbara, California to Baja California. *Habitat*: Among algae in the rocky intertidal and offshore on kelp; intertidal to 93 m (305 ft). *Remarks*: A quick and agile spider crab. It is highly dependent on kelp beds for food and shelter, and populations in the San Diego area have not yet recovered from the drastic reductions in kelp caused by the large El Niño of the early 1980's.

25. *Epialtoides hiltoni*

Winged kelp crab

Identification: A distinctive species with a maple-leaf shaped carapace and all carapace projections rounded. Claw of male with an extremely long propodus. *Size*: Males to 15.7 mm (0.6 in) in width; females 9.6 mm (0.4 in). *Range*: Laguna Beach, California to Baja California. *Habitat*: Found at the base of algae, surfgrass, and eelgrass in the low intertidal zone; also subtidally among shell rubble. Remarks: This small crab has rarely been collected, possibly because it is so cryptic or is mistaken for the juvenile of another species.

26. *Podochela hemphilli*

Hemphill's kelp crab

Identification: Rostrum terminates in a single point; carapace triangular, with no spines near the eyes. First pair of walking legs exceptionally long and adorned with numerous curved hairs. Claws of adult males very stout, with an unusually swollen, curved merus. *Size*: Males to 22.4 mm (0.9 in) and females to 11.5 mm (0.4 in). *Range*: Central California to Panama. *Habitat*: Found on pilings and also dredged from mud, sand, and rock bottoms; from the intertidal to 150 m (490 ft). *Remarks*: This small crab can virtually be identified by the pattern of its decorations, which are concentrated on the outer half of the long first pair of walking legs. When frightened it often raises one of these legs and holds it horizontally between itself and the perceived threat.

27. *Pyromaia tuberculata*

Tuberculate pear crab

Identification: Carapace pear-shaped, bearing several large tubercles and having a strong, curved spine immediately behind the eye; rostrum ending in a single point. Claws shorter than the first pair of walking legs. *Size*: To 17.7 mm (0.7 in). *Range*: Tomales Bay, California to Columbia; introduced to Japan and western Australia. *Habitat*: Found under rocks in the intertidal zone of sheltered bays and on pilings, and subtidal to 411 m (1350 ft). *Remarks*: Primarily subtidal, but readily accessible on pilings and the undersides of floats where it can be seen slowly picking its way through the encrusting organisms. It first appeared in Japan in the early 1970's, having probably been transported there either on the hulls of ships or as larvae in their ballast water.

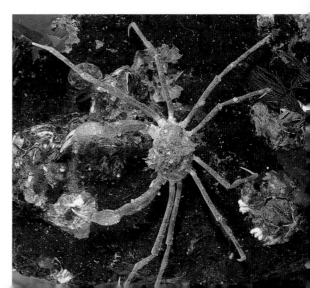

28. *Erileptus spinosus*

Identification: One of three spider crabs on our coast that has a rostrum ending in a single point. Adult males are easily distinguished from the other two species by their slender claws that are much longer than the first pair of walking legs, instead of only half the length. Females can be recognized by the strong spine above each eye which is absent in the other species. **Size**: Tiny, with a maximum recorded carapace width of 7.8 mm (0.3 in). **Range**: Santa Rosa Island, California to Panama. **Habitat**: Usually associated with shell rubble on sand or mud bottoms. Recorded from 4-548 m (12-1800 ft). **Remarks**: Males and females are so different in appearance that they were once classified in separate genera. They have been observed extending their legs into currents and feeding on the particles that become trapped among the hairs on their legs.

29. *Mimulus foliatus*

Foliate kelp crab

Identification: Our only spider crab (with the exception of the very dissimilar *Chionoecetes* [11]) whose carapace is wider than it is long. Lateral carapace teeth formed into flattened, slightly overlapping expansions. Color and pattern extremely variable, ranging from white or brown to yellow, orange, or bright red. **Size**: Males to 42 mm* (1.6 in); females 32.4 mm (1.2 in). **Range**: Dutch Harbor, Alaska to San Diego, California. **Habitat**: Primarily found in the shallow subtidal but ranges from the low intertidal to 128 m (420 ft). Lives in and around kelp holdfasts and in crevices; limited to areas on or near the open coast. **Remarks**: Although sometimes encrusted with organisms, this species decorates very little, relying instead on its coloration for protection. It feeds primarily on drifting pieces of kelp.

Family CHEIRAGONIDAE

30. *Telmessus cheiragonus*

Helmet crab

Identification: Lateral margin of carapace with six large, jagged teeth on each side; entire body surface covered with stiff, bristly hairs. Color predominantly yellowish green; fingers of claws dark. **Size**: To 102 mm (4 in). **Range**: Norton Sound, Alaska to Monterey, California; Siberia to Japan. Rare south of Puget Sound. **Habitat**: Intertidal to 110 m (360 ft). Usually found subtidally in or near eelgrass beds but sometimes ventures onto rocks with heavy algal cover. **Remarks**: An active crab that will often run at the approach of a diver. The abundance of these odd crabs in a given area seems to fluctuate tremendously, but this may be due to burial since captive specimens will sometimes completely disappear into the sediment for long periods of time.

Family CANCRIDAE

31. *Cancer magister*

Dungeness crab

Identification: Carapace widest at the tenth and very prominent final tooth following the eye; claws with white tips and serrated along the upper margin of the palm and finger. Color and pattern varies little except for slight differences in the amount and intensity of purple on the claws and legs. *Size*: To 230 mm (9 in), but usually less than 190 mm (7.5 in). There is one old report of specimens measuring 330 mm (13 in)! *Range*: Pribilof Islands to Santa Barbara, California. *Habitat*: Most common subtidally on sandy bottoms and in eelgrass beds; occurs from the low intertidal to 230 m (750 ft). Juveniles can be extremely abundant in the intertidal zone. *Remarks*: Diet consists primarily of clams, but also feeds on smaller crustaceans and fish. During the daytime it often remains buried with only the eyes and antennae exposed. This species supports important sport and commercial fisheries, with commercial quantities occurring from Kodiak, Alaska to central California.

32. *Cancer productus*

Red rock crab

Identification: Carapace teeth somewhat broad and rounded, with teeth between eyes of nearly equal size and shape. Claws large, with black tips. Adults are typically a uniform reddish color, while juveniles are extremely variable and often have very striking "zebra" patterns. *Size*: Males to 200 mm (7.8 in); females 158 mm (6.2 in). *Range*: Kodiak, Alaska to Isla San Martin, Baja California. *Habitat*: Found from the middle intertidal to 79 m (260 ft). Occurs on a wide range of substrate types, but is most common in gravelly areas and on well-protected boulder beaches. *Remarks*: This crab is a voracious predator, using its powerful claws to open clams, snails, mussels, and barnacles, and to catch smaller crabs. It is collected by sport crabbers but has attracted little commercial attention to date.

adult
juveniles

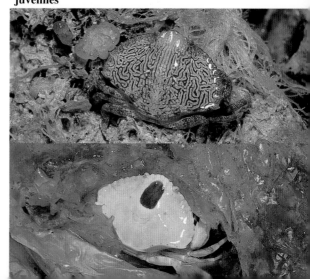

33. *Cancer anthonyi*

Yellow crab

Identification: Carapace smooth, hairless, and slightly domed. Claws black-tipped, the black extending less than halfway up the top edge of the moveable finger; orange blotch on inside of claw. Carapace and legs a uniform orange-yellow. *Size*: Males to 176 mm (6.9 in); females 144 mm (5.6 in). *Range*: Humboldt Bay, California to Bahia Magdalena, Baja California. *Habitat*: Found on open sand bottoms in southern California and largely confined to and bays and estuaries in the northern part of its range. Recorded from the low intertidal to 132 m (433 ft), but most abundant from 20-55 m (60-180 ft) on sand. *Remarks*: Along with the Pacific rock crab *C. antennarius* [35] this species supports a minor commercial and recreational fishery along the southern California coast.

34. *Cancer gracilis*

Graceful crab

Identification: Often mistaken for a Dungeness crab, *C. magister* [31], it can be distinguished from its much larger relative by the shape of its carapace (which is widest at the ninth tooth instead of the tenth), the white edging of the carapace teeth, and the lack of serrations on the upper margin of the claws. Claws with white tips; legs purple. *Size*: Males to 115 mm (4.5 in); females 87 mm (3.4 in). *Range*: Prince William Sound, Alaska to Bahia Playa Maria, Mexico. *Habitat*: Primarily subtidal on sand or mud and preferring slightly muddier areas than *C. magister*; cannot tolerate low salinity water so is usually absent from estuaries. Recorded from the low intertidal to 143 m (470 ft). *Remarks*: Feeds on small bivalves and barnacles and is sometimes considered a pest on commercial oyster beds. Megalopae and small juveniles can often be found clinging to large jellyfish, presumably using them for transport to nearshore areas.

35. *Cancer antennarius*

Pacific rock crab

Identification: Easily distinguished from other Pacific coast *Cancer* crabs by the conspicuous red spotting on the underside of the body. Claws large, black tipped; carapace reddish-brown. Juveniles usually have a dense covering of hair on the carapace. *Size*: Males to 178 mm (7 in); females 148 mm (5.8 in). *Range*: Queen Charlotte Sound, British Columbia to Cabo San Lucas, Mexico. *Habitat*: Found under boulders in the low intertidal, subtidally in kelp beds, and on gravel bottoms to 91 m (300 ft) but usually at depths less than 45 m (150 ft). Most abundant subtidally near rock-sand interfaces along exposed coastlines. *Remarks*: Although perceived as being a southern species, this crab is quite common in Barkley Sound on the west side of Vancouver Island, British Columbia.

36. *Cancer oregonensis*

Pygmy rock crab

Identification: Carapace nearly circular in outline and widest at seventh or eighth tooth following the eye; dorsal surface sometimes ornamented with raised, wartlike protuberances. Color usually brownish-red or orange but white, mottled, or striped specimens common in some areas. Claw tips black; legs very hairy. *Size*: To 53 mm (2 in). *Range*: Pribilof Islands to Palos Verdes, California; uncommon south of Pt. Arena, California. *Habitat*: Found under rocks in the low intertidal zone and especially abundant subtidally, tucked inside empty giant barnacle shells. Reported to 436 m (1430 ft). *Remarks*: This stout little crab uses its rounded carapace to block the opening of the hole that it inhabits. It is primarily active at night, emerging to feed on small barnacles.

37. *Cancer branneri*

Furrowed rock crab

Identification: The only Pacific coast *Cancer* having dark-tipped claws that bear spines along the upper margin of the moveable finger. Walking legs and surface of carapace very hairy; color usually a variable mosaic of red, orange, white, and purple. *Size*: Males to 58 mm (2.3 in); females 62 mm* (2.4 in). *Range*: Granite Cove, Alaska to Isla de Cedros, Baja California. *Habitat*: Found subtidally on gravel and especially shell, to 179 m (587 ft); rarely reported from the intertidal. Appears limited to areas on or near the open coast. *Remarks*: This small, active crab was formerly called *C. gibbosulus*. Like many other *Cancer* crabs it often buries in the substrate, leaving only its eyes and antennae visible.

38. *Cancer jordani*

Hairy rock crab

Identification: Carapace teeth strongly curved; surface of carapace and legs very hairy. Fingers of claws black-tipped, with no spines on the upper margin of the moveable finger. Color dark brown or reddish, often mottled. *Size*: Males to 39.3 mm* (1.5 in); females 19.5 mm (0.7 in). *Range*: Neah Bay, Washington to Bahia de Tortuga, Baja California; rare north of Oregon. *Habitat*: Found under rocks in the low intertidal of bays and subtidally in kelp holdfasts, to 104 m (340 ft). *Remarks*: Another small species with black-tipped claws, the bigtooth rock crab, *C. amphioetus*, is occasionally collected in southern California. It can be recognized by its very broad and blunt carapace teeth and the absence of hair on the carapace.

29

Family PINNOTHERIDAE

39. *Fabia subquadrata*

Mussel crab

Identification: Adults pass through two stages so dissimilar they were once classified into different genera. The hard-shelled planktonic form has walking legs densely fringed with hair for swimming and a thick "brow" along the front of the carapace, while those living inside a host mussel have a membranous carapace with distinctive narrow grooves extending back from each eye. *Size*: Males to 7.3 mm (0.3 in); females 22 mm (0.8 in). *Range*: Akutan Pass, Alaska to Ensenada, Baja California. *Habitat*: Intertidal to 220 m (720 ft). Adult females found singly inside the mussel *Modiolus modiolus*; occasionally in other bivalves. *Remarks*: After settling out of the plankton, juveniles enter a molluscan host. At sexual maturity, they are transformed into the hardshelled swimming stage that leaves the host to mate in the plankton; the males then apparently die while the females reenter mussels where they remain for life, again becoming soft-bodied and producing broods from that single mating.

b.

40. *Scleroplax granulata*

Burrow pea crab

Identification: Carapace oval in outline and very hard and smooth. Males with unusually large, thick claws. Color pale grey or brown; cornea of eye bright red. *Size*: To 12.9 mm (0.5 in). *Range*: Porcher Island, British Columbia to Ensenada, Baja California. *Habitat*: Middle intertidal to 55 m (180 ft) in sand, mud, or sandy gravel. Commensal in the burrows of the ghost shrimp, *Neotrypaea* [158], mud shrimp, Upog*ebia* [160], and the fat inkeeper worm, *Urechus caupo*. *Remarks*: Feeds on detritus and leftover food scraps from the host and can also filter feed using its maxillipeds.

41. *Pinnixa faba*

Mantle pea crab

Identification: Males hard-bodied while females are quite soft. Outer margin of orbit of female rounded and claws without a gape when closed. Male with a tooth near the base of the movable finger. Color variable, ranging from white to orange and male often with dark markings. *Size*: Males to 17.5 mm (0.7 in); females 25 mm (1 in). *Range*: Prince of Wales Island, Alaska to Newport Beach, California. *Habitat*: Found inside the horse clam, *Tresus capax*; juveniles often in other species of clam. *Remarks*: Although several crabs may be found inside a clam, only one pair is sexually mature. They feed by intercepting food-laden mucous strands and their activities cause some slight damage to the host.

42. *Pinnixa littoralis*

Gaper pea crab

Identification: Females easier to distinguish from *P. faba* [41] than are males, having pointed outer margins on the orbit of the eye and claws that gape when closed. Third walking leg of male proportionately much larger than that of *P. faba* and the claw lacks the tooth near the base of the movable finger. Both sexes white; males often with darker markings. *Size*: Male to 18 mm (0.7 in); female 27 mm (1 in). *Range*: Prince William Sound, Alaska to Bahia Santa Maria, Baja California. *Habitat*: Found in the mantle cavity of the horse clam, *Tresus capax*, from the intertidal to 91 m (300 ft). Juveniles sometimes found in other bivalves. *Remarks*: Relatively scarce in the Puget Sound region compared to *P. faba*.

43. *Pinnixa tubicola*

Identification: Carapace smooth and rectangular in outline. Propodus of the enlarged third walking leg is greatly expanded relative to the dactyl. *Size*: Males to 10 mm (0.4 in); females 18 mm* (0.7 in). *Range*: Prince Rupert, British Columbia to San Diego, California. *Habitat*: Lives in the tubes of *Chaetopterus* and terebellid worms, from the low intertidal to 57 m (187 ft). *Remarks*: One of the more common of several very similar pea crabs that inhabit worm tubes or burrows and that usually need to be examined under magnification for positive identification.

44. *Opisthopus transversus*

Mottled pea crab

Identification: Carapace smooth and shiny, only slightly wider than long, and often mottled with red. Walking legs stout, very hairy, and fairly uniform in size. *Size*: Males to 11.8 mm (0.4 in); females 21 mm (0.8 in). *Range*: Monterey, California to Laguna San Ignacio, Baja California and Gulf of California. *Habitat*: Recorded from wide variety of intertidal and subtidal hosts including clams, sea cucumbers, snails, polychaetes, and sea slugs. *Remarks*: Another southern California pea crab, *Pinnixa barnharti*, also lives inside the sweet potato cucumber, *Caudina arenicola*. The third pair of walking legs are noticeably longer and stouter than the other legs.

45. *Pinnotheres pugettensis*

Identification: Carapace very soft and membranous and about equal in length and width. Last three pairs of walking legs with a dense fringe of hairs. *Size*: To 13 mm (0.5 in). *Range*: Spider Anchorage, British Columbia to Monterey, California. *Habitat*: Found inside large tunicates, particularly *Halocynthia* in the north and *Styela* in the south; also recorded from the rock scallop, *Hinnites giganteus*. From 6-64 m (20-210 ft). *Remarks*: A second member of the genus, *P. taylori*, also occurs in tunicates in Washington and British Columbia. It typically has a pair of small tubercles near the middle of the carapace.

Alex Kerstitch

Family PORTUNIDAE

46. *Portunus xantusii*

Xantus' swimming crab

Identification: Last pair of walking legs formed into flattened paddles for swimming; lateral carapace spines very long and sharp. Inner margin of carpus of claw ending with a prominent spine. Color predominantly gray with some red or purple on the fingers of the claws; carapace sometimes with white markings. *Size*: To 73 mm (2.8 in). *Range*: Santa Barbara, California to Topolobampo, Mexico. *Habitat*: On sand or in eelgrass beds, from the low intertidal to 179 m (590 ft). *Remarks*: A quick, predatory crab that has been observed preying on sand crabs, *Emerita* [155]. Commonly seen during night dives over sandy bottoms, where it tends to run or swim a short distance when disturbed and then rapidly bury.

47. *Callinectes arcuatus*

Arched swimming crab

Identification: Carapace with six teeth between eyes, the innermost pair much smaller than the rest. Inner margin of carpus of claw without a spine. Color a bluish-green, with blue legs. *Size*: Males to 146.4 mm (5.7 in); females 124 mm (4.9 in). *Range:* Los Angeles to Peru. *Habitat* Found in estuaries on sand or mud, from the intertidal to 150 ft. *Remarks:* A very similar species, *C. bellicosus*, has been reported from the San Diego area. The anterior surface of the carapace lacks the numerous granules present on *C. arcuatus*.

48. *Callinectes sapidus*

Blue crab

Identification: Can be distinguished from the native *C. arcuatus* by the four equal teeth between the eyes. Color gray or bluish-green with red on the spines; females with bright red fingers. *Size*: Carapace width to 209 mm (8.2 in). *Range*: Native to the Atlantic, where it ranges from Nova Scotia to Uruguay. Pacific coast sightings to date have been limited to San Francisco Bay, where it was very recently accidentally or intentionally introduced. *Habitat*: An estuarine species that can tolerate fresh water. *Remarks*: By far the most economically important crab on the east coast of the U.S., where newly-molted specimens are marketed as softshell crabs.

49. *Carcinus maenas*

European green crab

Identification: Carapace with five large teeth following the eye; last pair of legs only slightly flattened. Carapace dull greenish with yellowish spotting; underside of body may be orange or reddish. *Size:* Males to 100 mm (3.9 in); females 79 mm (3.1 in). *Range:* Native to Europe but widely introduced, with populations in Australia, South Africa, and both coasts of North America. The founders of the west coast population may have come in with algae used as packing material for live lobsters or baitworms shipped from the east coast. Since appearing in San Francisco Bay in 1989, it has been found as far south as Morro Bay, California and north to Clayoquot Sound, Vancouver Island, British Columbia. *Habitat:* Found in sand, mud, or vegetation in very shallow water. *Remarks:* West coast populations are extremely limited in their habitat use compared to those in other parts of the world, occurring primarily in high intertidal salt marshes and warm sloughs lacking larger native crabs (*e.g., Cancer productus [32]*) that readily prey on them. Juvenile green crabs appear to have difficulty competing with native grapsids for space under rocks.

Family GONEPLACIDAE

50. *Malacoplax californiensis*

California burrowing crab

Identification: Carapace nearly rectangular in outline; claws black-tipped. Legs, carapace, and even eyestalks fringed with hair. *Size*: Carapace width to 31.3 mm (1.2 in). *Range*: Morro Bay, California to Baja California. *Habitat*: Builds burrows in the middle and low intertidal of muddy bays and estuaries and also reported to hide under objects on mud flats. Recorded subtidally to 33 m (108 ft). Remarks: Reportedly common in the early part of this century, this small crab now appears to be virtually extinct in the U.S.

33

Marc Chamberlain

Family OCYPODIDAE
51. *Uca crenulata*

Mexican fiddler

Identification: Carapace somewhat rectangular in outline; eyestalks extremely long, folding laterally into grooves along the front margin of carapace. Males with one claw greatly enlarged. *Size*: To 19.7 mm (0.7 in). *Range*: Goleta Slough, California to Baja California. Marinas and other shoreline construction has destroyed most of this species' habitat in southern California and it is now fairly rare in the U.S. *Habitat*: Builds permanent burrows as much as 1.2 m (4 ft) deep in the high and middle intertidal sand and mud flats of bays and estuaries. *Remarks*: Males use their single enlarged claw to attract females and in contests against other males. The small claws are used to transfer sediment to the mouth where edible organic material and tiny organisms are sorted and ingested, and the discarded pellets of processed mud left scattered near the mouths of their burrows.

Family LEUCOSIIDAE
52. *Randallia ornata*

Purple globe crab

Identification: Carapace very round and bulbous, with a granular texture and armed with two pairs of short but distinct projections along the posterior margin. Color usually white with purple or red blotches and spots. *Size*: Carapace width to at least 53.2 mm (2 in). *Range*: Mendocino County, California to Bahia Magdalena, Baja California. *Habitat*: Found on open sand bottoms. Although found on rare occasions intertidally, it is typically a subtidal form that occurs down to 92 m (300 ft). *Remarks*: Remains buried in sand during the day.

Family PARTHENOPIDAE
53. *Heterocrypta occidentalis*

Sandflat elbow crab

Identification: This bizarre crab, with its triangular carapace and extremely long claws terminating in tiny pincers, cannot be mistaken for any other species on our coast. Color pink to white, often with purple markings on raised areas. *Size*: Carapace width to 21 mm (0.8 in). *Range*: Marin County, California to the Gulf of California. *Habitat*: Recorded from the low intertidal to 174 m (570 ft), but typically found from 8-103 m (25-340 ft) on sand bottoms. *Remarks*: Usually remains buried in sand during the daytime, leaving only the rostrum and eyes showing. Specimens in captivity are carnivorous and capture prey between the propodus and carpus of the claw rather than using the small pincers.

Caridea

Shrimps are most familiar to us as the main course of a seafood dinner or as tiny curled tails sprinkled on salad. While very attractive in a culinary sense, this form provides no hint of the delicate beauty, grace, and color of the living animals. Only a handful of Pacific coast shrimps grow large enough to attract our attention as food, yet this area is home to an incredible variety of smaller species that are important prey of many fish, birds, and other animals. This nearly universal appreciation of shrimp dinners has forced shrimps to adopt a number of strategies to postpone such encounters. One of the best known of these is the so-called "caridean escape response", a very effective behavior that has also been adopted by many non-shrimps like lobsters and crayfish. By forcefully snapping the abdomen down and underneath, the animal propels itself backwards using the large surface area of the flattened tail fan to push against the water. Such a mechanism requires a lot of muscle to be effective, and it is precisely that heavily muscled abdomen that makes them so desirable as food.

If the initial escape attempt fails, the shrimp may resort to other tactics. When captured, some of the spinier shrimps bend their abdomens dorsally toward their heads in what has been called the "cataleptic" position, exposing spines along the lower edges of their abdomens and presumably making them much more difficult for a predator to swallow. Similarly, the long, sharp, toothed rostrums of many shrimps aid in defense by reducing the number of possible ways a small fish can swallow them, and shrimp sometimes escape when the fish tries to reposition them for swallowing. Some species flare out their antennal scales (Fig. 7a) to expose the spines at their tips and make them harder to ingest, and anyone who has handled large, live prawns barehanded can attest to the sharpness of their rostrums and telsons.

Not all shrimps are armed with long rostrums and this feature is very much correlated with habitat. Those that spend much of their time concealed beneath rocks and in crevices tend to have short rostrums and stockier bodies; long rostrums are presumably impractical in such close confines and these species only emerge after dark when there is less risk of fish predation. Conversely, those living in more exposed locations such as on open mud or in eelgrass and algae do not have as effective a refuge from daytime predators and typically have very long, sharp rostrums and a more slender build.

Whether concealed beneath rocks or living among algae, most of the smaller shrimps are cryptically colored. Those living among algae often exactly match the color of their surroundings, so that within a single species there may be bright red, green, or brown individuals depending on the kind of seaweeds with which they are associated. As a general rule these tend to have a fairly uniform coloration while those living among rock and shell show more variation in color and pattern. One common pattern, for example, is an ivory-white carapace and a bright green abdomen; such "disruptive coloration" serves to break up the outline of the shrimp and make it difficult to distinguish from its surroundings. If all specimens looked like this a fish might soon learn to key on it, but odds are the next shrimp it encounters will have an entirely different pattern. Female shrimp are often more strongly colored than males, and this is probably due to the different responsibilities of the sexes in reproduction. While the males of some species can get away with being largely transparent, females must conceal both the developing ovary beneath their carapace and the eggs on their pleopods during brooding. By keeping both the carapace and side plates of the abdomen an opaque, cryptic color, they can keep both the ovary and eggs hidden from view, an important consideration since both typically go through considerable color changes over the course of their development.

Although shrimps are not usually thought of as having claws, all species found on the Pacific coast have at least one pair of small pincers used for grooming and to handle food and the different families of shrimps can be easily recognized by the size, shape, and position of these limbs. The **Crangonidae** (pg. 39) are the only family having *subchelate* claws, these differ from *chelate* appendages in that the moveable finger closes flat against the hand rather than against a fixed finger (Fig. 7b). Crangonids tend to be more flattened than other shrimps and generally bury in sand or mud. Using their legs and pleopods they can sink out of sight in seconds, leaving only their eyes and antennae visible. A few broad sweeps of the long antennae put the finishing touches on the job by brushing over and erasing the slight remaining impression left by the body. In this position they are both well-protected from predators and can also ambush passing prey: smaller crustaceans, worms, and even fish are seized by the subchelate first pair of legs and swallowed whole. Many crangonids emerge at night to search for food and some species enter the water column in pursuit of mysids and other small organisms. Divers are most likely to spot them during night dives over sandy bottoms, but even when these shrimps are out in the open they are easily overlooked because they often match both the color and pattern of the substrate.

Crangonids are caught for human consumption in Europe, but their relatively small size has attracted little attention along the Pacific coast. At one time some of the larger species supported a commercial fishery in San Francisco Bay, but those taken now are primarily sold as bait. In addition to being important prey for many species of fish they are also the main food of newly-weaned harbor seals.

Unlike good children, the **Alpheidae** (pg. 42) are heard but not seen. The best known members of this family are the snapping or pistol shrimps, which have a specially modified and often greatly enlarged claw capable of producing a very loud popping sound. The pop of a large shrimp can break glass that has been previously scratched, and the concussion can reportedly stun small fish so that they can be captured by the shrimp. In many tropical areas and even some parts of southern California, the continuous crackling sound of thousands of these small shrimps firing their salvos is very noticeable underwater and sounds much like food being fried in hot oil.

Not all of the members of this family are noisemakers, however. Shrimps of the genus *Betaeus* also have unusually large but conventional claws that lack the unusual mechanism found in the snapping shrimps. These small shrimp almost invariably live in close association with some larger animal and along our coast the hosts include sea urchins, abalone, porcelain crabs, and ghost shrimp. Like their noisy cousins they appear to be exceptionally long-lived for shrimp, with specimens that were collected as adults living for many years in captivity. Members of this group are sometimes called "hooded shrimp" because the front edge of their carapace extends over their eyes.

The **Hippolytidae** (pg. 45) contains far more species than any other family on our coast. These include the common "broken-back" shrimps found under rocks and in tidepools, along with many subtidal forms living on both rocky and soft bottoms. One of the characters used in identification keys for these shrimps is whether the end segment (dactyl) of the walking legs are simple or bifid (Fig. 7c). In addition to being a handy taxonomic character this structure provides some insight into the type of habitat the animal lives in, simple dactyls being typical of soft bottoms and bifid ones for rock and algae.

Unlike alpheids, they have prominent rostrums, but the two families share the character of having larger claws on first pair of legs than on the second and the 'wrist' or carpus of the second pair of legs subdivided to form a flexible appendage for grooming and reaching into small crevices. Almost all Pacific coast hippolytids have 7 of these subdivisions with the only exceptions being *Hippolyte* with three and *Lysmata* with about 30.

Superficially similar to the hippolytids, but having the larger claws on the second pair of legs rather than on the first, are the **Palaemonidae** (pg. 52). This is primarily a tropical family having only a few representatives that barely make it up into southern California; the only one occurring farther north is the oriental shrimp *Palaemon macrodactylus* which was accidently introduced into San Francisco Bay and has recently appeared in Willapa Bay on the Washington coast.

The commercially-important Pacific coast shrimps belong to the **Pandalidae** (pg. 53). All have long, upturned rostrums and lack claws on their first pair of legs; the second pair has very tiny pincers and the carpus is subdivided into twenty or more articulations. Although lacking large claws some pandalids are still quite adept at capturing smaller organisms, even shrimp, by caging them between their long legs. Several species move up into the water column at night to feed. Pandalids are protandric hermaphrodites, meaning all begin adult life as males and later change sex to female. The size and age at which this occurs is partially

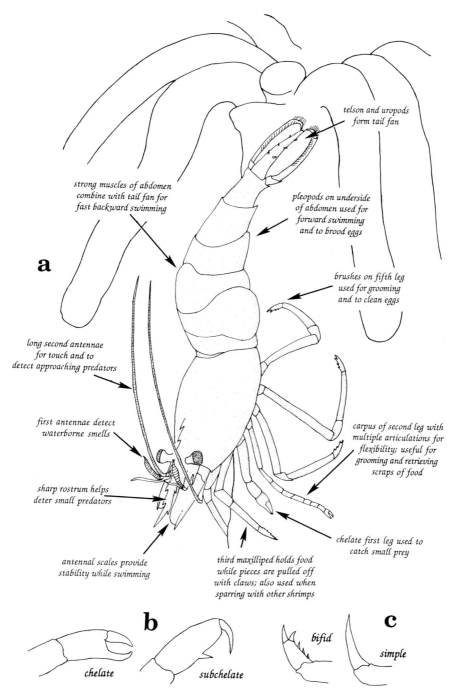

a

telson and uropods
form tail fan

strong muscles of abdomen
combine with tail fan for
fast backward swimming

pleopods on underside
of abdomen used for
forward swimming
and to brood eggs

brushes on fifth leg
used for grooming
and to clean eggs

long second antennae
for touch and to
detect approaching predators

first antennae detect
waterborne smells

carpus of second leg with
multiple articulations for
flexibility; useful for
grooming and retrieving
scraps of food

sharp rostrum helps
deter small predators

chelate first leg used to
catch small prey

antennal scales provide
stability while swimming

third maxilliped holds food
while pieces are pulled off
with claws; also used when
sparring with other shrimps

b   **c**

chelate   *subchelate*   *bifid*   *simple*

Figure 7. (a) Hippolytid shrimp; (b) chelate and subchelate appendages; (c) bifid and simple dactyls.

37

dependant on the density of females in the population, with sex change occuring at a smaller size if few females are around and being delayed if many large females are already present.

   Most pandalids live on fairly open, soft bottoms and are fished using trawls; because of their small size they are typically canned or frozen as "cocktail" shrimp. The most notable exception is the spot shrimp (*Pandalus platyceros*) which lives in rockier areas and is caught in baited pots. Often marketed as a "prawn", it should not be confused with the large breaded penaeid shrimp tails so common to seafood platters, frozen food sections, and similar habitats. These are either caught in the Gulf of Mexico or imported, and although west coast pandalids are a resource of considerable economic importance, their landings are only a small fraction of the value of Gulf Coast penaeids.

Pictorial key to Hippolytid shrimp.

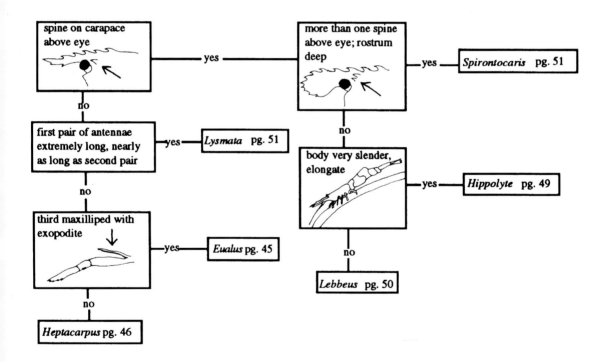

Family CRANGONIDAE

54. *Paracrangon echinata*
Horned shrimp

Identification: A bizarre and atypical crangonid that is missing the second pair of legs entirely. The rostrum is long and sharp and the carapace and abdomen very spiny; when disturbed it assumes the cataleptic position. Color is a uniform yellowish to pale brown. *Size*: To about 70 mm (2.7 in). *Range*: Port Etches, Alaska to La Jolla, California. *Habitat*: Most abundant among hydroids, bryozoans, and worm tubes on mixed composition bottoms, from 7-201 m (23-660 ft). Unlike most other crangonids, it does not bury. *Remarks*: Feeds on smaller crustaceans and worms that are ambushed and swallowed whole. The extremely slender third pair of legs are held just above the substrate and function as antennae to detect prey, which are then seized and subdued with the subchelate first pair of legs.

55. *Mesocrangon munitella*
Miniature spinyhead

Identification: Carapace with two dorsal spines and three spines on each side. Fifth segment of abdomen sharply tapered; sixth segment narrow. Highly variable in color and markings. *Size*: Total length to 23 mm (0.9 in). *Range*: Queen Charlotte Sound, British Columbia to Punta Eugenia, Baja California. *Habitat*: Found in the low intertidal and subtidally to 73 m (240 ft) on silty sand and especially mixed composition bottoms, where the varying patterns of light and dark blend in well with shell fragments and gravel. *Remarks*: This diminutive and well-camouflaged shrimp is nearly impossible to find in the daytime unless one drags a fine-meshed net over the bottom, but can often be spotted at night when it emerges to feed on smaller organisms.

56. *Metacrangon munita*
Coastal spinyhead

Identification: Carapace with large, often hairy depressions and two dorsal spines and two spines on each side. Appendages also very hairy. Coloration shown is typical, with a very dark carapace and a prominent white "saddle" on the abdomen. *Size*: Length to 48 mm (1.9 in). *Range*: Port Etches, Alaska to San Miguel Island, California. *Habitat*: Subtidal on sand-shell and mixed composition bottoms, from 13-230 m (42-750 ft). *Remarks*: Spends much of its time buried and is likely to be seen only during night dives.

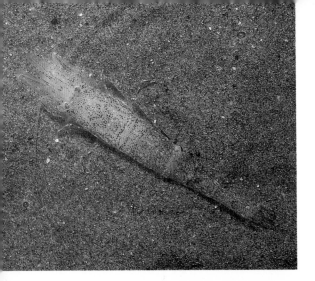

57. *Crangon franciscorum*

California bay shrimp

Identification: Distinguished by the unusually long subchelate hand of the first leg and the spine on each side of the upper rear margin of the fifth abdominal segment. Carapace with a single median dorsal spine. There are two subspecies: *C. f. franciscorum* (pictured) has a hand 4 - 5.5 times longer than wide, while *C. f. angustimana* has an even more exaggerated claw in which the length is 6 - 8 times greater than the width. *Size*: Length to 84 mm (3.3 in). *Range*: Resurrection Bay, Alaska to San Diego, California. *Habitat*: The more commonly encountered *C. f. franciscorum* is an estuarine form, sometimes occurring in nearly fresh water and recorded from the intertidal to 91 m (300 ft). *C. f. angustimana* occurs in deeper, higher salinity water, from 18-183 m (60-600 ft). *Remarks*: Feeds on smaller crustaceans such as shrimp and mysids, and also on small bivalves and polychaetes.

58. *Crangon nigricauda*

Blacktail shrimp

Identification: A very stocky *Crangon* having a single median carapace spine and a shallow groove on the underside of the sixth segment of the abdomen. Antennal scale shorter than the telson, with the blade fairly broad at the tip and projecting forward as far or nearly as far as the spine. *Size*: To 53 mm (2 in). *Range*: Prince William Sound, Alaska to Isla San Geronimo, Baja California, Mexico. *Habitat*: Found on sandy and mixed composition bottoms and around eelgrass beds. Common intertidally and recorded to 57 m (187 ft). *Remarks*: Despite the name, the color of the tail can be quickly changed and is often not black. The diet consists largely of amphipods.

59. *Crangon alaskensis*

Northern crangon

Identification: Like *C. nigricauda* [58], this species has one median carapace spine and a groove beneath the sixth segment of the abdomen, but it has a much more slender build. The blade of the antennal scale is narrower and does not extend as far forward as the spine, and the antennal scale is as long or longer than the telson. *Size*: Total length to 65 mm (2.5 in). *Range*: Bering Sea to San Diego, California. *Habitat*: Found on sandy bottoms, from the intertidal to 275 m (900 ft). *Remarks*: *C. alaskensis* and *C. nigricauda* are both abundant and occur together in Puget Sound, and specimens appearing to have intermediate characters between the two may be hybrids.

60. *Crangon nigromaculata*

Blackspotted shrimp

Identification: One of the easiest members of the genus to identify in the field because of the conspicuous blue "eyespot" on each side of the sixth segment of the abdomen. Carapace with a single dorsal spine. *Size*: Length to about 70 mm (2.7 in). *Range*: Northern California to Baja California. *Habitat*: Found on sand bottoms from 5-174 m (16-565 ft). *Remarks*: This species, along with the more abundant *C. nigricauda* [58] and *C. franciscorum* [57], was once fished commercially in San Francisco Bay.

61. *Crangon stylirostris*

Smooth bay shrimp

Identification: A rather stocky *Crangon* and our only member of the genus lacking a dorsal carapace spine. Coloration largely matches the sand in their habitat. *Size*: To 61 mm (2.4 in). *Range*: Chirikof Island, Alaska to San Luis Obispo Bay, California. *Habitat*: Found intertidally on fairly high energy, wave swept beaches and subtidally to 80 m (262 ft) on hard sand or mixed rock and sand. *Remarks*: Much livelier and faster-moving than most of its relatives, probably an adaptation to the very rigorous habitat in which it lives. Feeds primarily on crustaceans and small clams.

62. *Crangon handi*

Identification: Body very short and stout; antennal scale broad and rounded with blade equal to or longer than spine. Carapace with single median dorsal spine. Color and pattern can be changed to match surroundings; tends to be more boldly marked with bands and spots than are other members of the genus. *Size*: To 50.3 mm (2 in). *Range*: Strait of Juan de Fuca, Washington* to Bahia Colnett, Baja California. Usually found subtidally south of Sonoma County. *Habitat*: Found on high-energy beaches where its bold patterning matches the coarse sand and shell, from the intertidal to 55 m (180 ft.) *Remarks*: In Washington, it occurs on very rocky beaches near the open coast, in the small patches of sand between and beneath boulders.

41

63. *Rhynocrangon alata*
Saddleback shrimp

Identification: A very stout, flattened, and knobby shrimp. Carapace with two dorsal spines and a short, upturned rostrum; outside edge of antennal scale concave. Third segment of abdomen with a very large dorsal hump. Color and pattern variable. *Size*: Total length to 45 mm (1.8 in). *Range*: Bering Sea to Pacific Grove, California. *Habitat*: Usually trawled from rocky areas at depths of 11-167 m (36-550 ft). *Remarks*: In captivity, this odd shrimp sits on rocks rather than burying in the sediment, and the pink "coralline algae" coloration of many specimens suggests that this may be their behavior in the wild.

64. *Sclerocrangon boreas*
Tank shrimp

Identification: A massive, heavily armored shrimp with three large dorsal carapace spines and a descending rostrum. Outer margin of antennal scale rounded; tip of third maxilliped flattened. Color and pattern variable. *Size*: Total length to 150 mm (5.9 in). *Range*: A circumboreal species, occurring from the Bering Sea to Washington but rarely seen in the southern part of its range. *Habitat*: Intertidal to 366 m (1200 ft), on coarse substrates. *Remarks*: Unique among Pacific coast shrimps in that it does not have free-swimming larval stages. The unusually large eggs hatch into small shrimp which, like freshwater crayfish, spend some time attached to the pleopods of the female.

Family ALPHEIDAE

65. *Betaeus macginitieae*
Urchin shrimp

Identification: A small, dark shrimp that lives underneath sea urchins. Claws large, with the fingers shorter than the palm. Color a very deep red to purple. *Size*: To at least 25 mm (1 in). *Range*: Monterey, California to Catalina Island. *Habitat*: Found underneath the sea urchins *Strongylocentrotus franciscanus* and *S. purpuratus*, in the low intertidal and subtidally. *Remarks*: Specimens removed from their host were able to find their way back, using both vision and their sense of smell. The similar abalone shrimp, *B. harfordi*, lives in the mantle cavity of abalone and is reported from Fort Bragg, California to Bahia Magdalena, Baja California. The claws are more rounded, with the fingers equal or slightly longer than the palm.

66. *Betaeus longidactylus*

Visored shrimp

Identification: Males (pictured) with exceptionally large claws; fingers longer than the palm. Color tends to be a dark blue or olive green, often with a white or tan dorsal stripe. *Size*: Length to 40 mm (1.5 in). *Range*: Elkhorn Slough to Bahia Tepoca, Mexico. *Habitat*: Found intertidally under rocks on protected and semiprotected beaches; also reported from sponges. *Remarks*: Although reported to associate with ghost shrimps, many appear to be free-living and sometimes occur in very large assemblages under rocks at low tide.

67. *Betaeus harrimani*

Northern hooded shrimp

Identification: Similar to the visored shrimp *B. longidactylus* [66] but distinguished by having the fingers of the claws shorter than the palm and having light-colored margins on the posterior edges of the abdominal segments. Color usually a dark blue or blue-gray dorsally and very pale along the sides of the carapace and abdomen. *Size*: Length to 35 mm (1.3 in). *Range*: Sitka, Alaska to Newport Bay, California. *Habitat*: Found intertidally in mud and sand, usually in the burrows of the mud shrimp, *Upogebia pugettensis* [160], and sometimes with *Neotrypaea californiensis* [158]. Occasionally appears to be free-living under debris. *Remarks*: Sometimes seen wandering in the open at night.

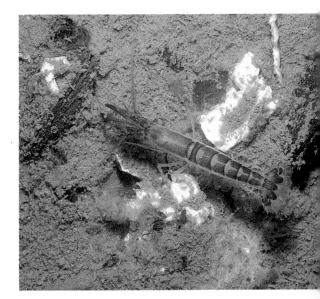

68. *Betaeus setosus*

Fuzzy hooded shrimp

Identification: Claws large and very rounded in outline; front margin of carapace with a prominent notch. Color a pale greenish-yellow. *Size*: To 25 mm (1 in). *Range*: Hecate Strait, British Columbia to Morro Bay, California. *Habitat*: Symbiotic with the thickclaw porcelain crab, *Pachycheles rudis* [147], often hiding directly beneath the pairs of crabs but easily overlooked due to its translucent coloration and tendency to remain motionless. Found from the low intertidal to 18 m (59 ft). *Remarks*: Often size-matched with the host pair of crabs, small ones living with small pairs while the largest shrimps cohabit with full-sized *Pachycheles*.

43

69. *Alpheus clamator*

Twistclaw pistol shrimp

Identification: Front of carapace with a prominent rostrum and much smaller, curved spines in front of each eye. Claws conspicuously blotched and spotted; tips of fingers orange. ***Size***: To 37 mm (1.4 in). ***Range***: Horseshoe Cove, Sonoma County, California to Bahia San Bartolome, Baja California. ***Habitat***: Lives in the low intertidal in burrows that it excavates under rocks and also in sponge cavities and kelp holdfasts. ***Remarks***: Usually lives in pairs, as does another southern California species, *A. californiensis*. This species occurs in burrows on mud flats and lacks the carapace spines by the eyes.

70. *Alpheus bellimanus*

Identification: Body a uniform blood red, but capable of quickly changing color to a pale olive green when captured. Snapping claw yellow with ivory blotches; small claw yellow with a broad expansion on the edge of the movable finger. ***Size***: Length to 23 mm (0.9 in). ***Range***: Monterey, California to the Galapagos. ***Habitat***: Found under rocks and in kelp holdfasts, ranging from the very low intertidal to 300 m (984 ft). ***Remarks***: The species name refers to the potent snap of the large claw (*belli* = war; *manus* = hand).

71. *Synalpheus lockingtoni*

Littoral pistol shrimp

Identification: Spines in front of each eye nearly as long as the rostrum; large claw long and smoothly rounded. Color of body and claws a uniform pale yellowish-green with fine reddish spotting. ***Size***: Length to 30 mm (1.2 in). ***Range***: Farallon Islands to Punta Marquez, Baja California. ***Habitat***: Found in the low intertidal and shallow subtidal, under rocks and among sessile invertebrates. ***Remarks***: Somewhat more aggressive in captivity than either *Alpheus clamator* [69] or *A. bellimanus* [70].

Family HIPPOLYTIDAE

72. *Eualus Lineatus*

Striped eualid

Identification: Boldly marked with broad reddish bands on a translucent background. This is our only member of the genus that has several small dorsal spines on the end of the first segment of the antennular peduncle. *Size:* Total length to about 25 mm (1 inch). *Range:* Juneau, Alaska to Santa Cruz Is., California *Habitat:* Subtidal; appears to be associated with sponges at depths of 12-120 m (39-390 ft.). *Remarks:* The broad red bands and multiple antennular spines readily distinguish this species from two similar forms, *E. pusiolus* and *E. subtilis*. The latter two can be difficult to identify in the field; they are most reliably separated by the multiple (2 to 5, usually 3) spines on the merus of the third walking of *E. subtilis*, versus a single spine in *E. pusiolus*.

73. *Eualus suckleyi*

Shortscale eualid

Identification: The fairly long, broad rostrum extends about as far forward as the end of the antennal scale. Abdomen with distinct red bands and reddish blotches in between the bands, and a small spine on the lower margin of the fourth segment. Antennae unbanded. *Size*: To 79 mm (3.1 in). *Range*: Chuckchi and Bering Sea to Grays Harbor, Washington; Okhotsk Sea. *Habitat*: Subtidal, from 11-1025 m (36-3360 ft). Usually on fairly soft bottoms. *Remarks*: Juveniles of this species can sometimes be found clinging to the columns of large plumose anemones, *Metridium giganteum**.

74. *Eualus townsendi*

Townsend's eualid

Identification: Structurally similar to *E. suckleyi* [73] but much more laterally compressed, with a prominent dorsal hump and lacking the red banding and the small spine on the bottom edge of the fourth segment of the abdomen. The antennae have widely-spaced but well-defined bands. *Size*: To 44 mm (1.7 in). *Range*: Pribilof Islands to Puget Sound. *Habitat*: Recorded from 38-630 m (124-2066 ft). *Remarks*: Color much like *Heptacarpus kincaidi* [78] and *H. tridens* [83] but differs from them in not having a white midrib on the rostrum and having more teeth on the carapace and rostrum, respectively.

75. *Heptacarpus brevirostris*
Stout shrimp

Identification: Named for its short rostrum that extends only as far as the cornea of the eye, ending in a single point with no ventral teeth. Color and pattern extremely variable, ranging from uniform browns or greens to various patterns of white mottling or stripes. *Size*: To 62 mm (2.4 in). *Range*: Attu, Aleutian Islands, Alaska to Santa Cruz, California. *Habitat*: Abundant on protected and semi-protected rocky beaches, under rocks in the daytime and roaming tidepools at night. Found from the middle intertidal to 128 m (420 ft). *Remarks*: Because it is large, common, and found in a wide range of habitats, this is probably the most frequently encountered intertidal shrimp along the northern Pacific coast. Adult males (pictured) have unusually long and stout third maxillipeds.

76. *Heptacarpus palpator*

Identification: Distinguished from *H. brevirostris* [75] by its longer rostrum, which extends beyond the cornea and has one or two ventral spines near the tip. Coloration variable but commonly brownish or with brown bands on a translucent background. *Size*: To 31 mm (1.2 in) *Range*: San Francisco Bay to Bahia Magdalena, Baja California; also Gulf of California. Usually found only in Monterey Bay and south of Point Conception. *Habitat*: Occurs under rocks in the low intertidal, in tidepools and among algae, and subtidally to 37 m (121 ft). *Remarks*: A third stout-bodied shrimp with a short rostrum is *H. taylori*, recorded from British Columbia through Baja California but rarely seen north of San Francisco. It has an extremely short, downcurved rostrum that does not reach as far forward as the cornea of the eye.

77. *Heptacarpus carinatus*
Smalleyed shrimp

Identification: Rostrum very long and straight and eyes disproportionately small. Third segment of abdomen with a prominent dorsal lobe. Color ranges from a bright green to reddish brown, often with a white dorsal stripe on the carapace. *Size*: To 60 mm* (2.3 in). *Range*: Dixon Harbor, Alaska to Point Loma, California. *Habitat*: Found in tidepools among algae and surfgrass, usually on or near the exposed coast. Reported from the low intertidal to 27 m (88 ft). *Remarks*: Strongly resembles the much smaller shrimps of the genus *Hippolyte* [85] both in appearance and behavior, using its short legs to cling tightly to surfgrass (*Phyllospadix*). Often occurs with the stiletto shrimp *Heptacarpus stylus* [82].

78. *Heptacarpus kincaidi*
Kincaid's shrimp

Identification: Easily recognized by its red and yellow markings and the distinctive white midrib of its rostrum. Third segment of the abdomen with a very prominent dorsal hump. *Size*: To 35 mm (1.3 in). *Range*: Discovery Passage, British Columbia to San Pedro, California. *Habitat*: Found on vertical rock walls and under ledges, in association with the crimson anemone, *Cribrinopsis fernaldi*. Depth range is 10-183 m (33-600 ft). *Remarks*: Usually clings to the base of the anemone or sits beneath the canopy of the tentacles, often in groups of a dozen or more. Sometimes associates with the painted anemone, *Urticina crassicornis*.

79. *Heptacarpus pugettensis*
Barred shrimp

Identification: Conspicuously marked with three broad, greenish-yellow bars on the inner ventral surface of the abdomen. Carapace and abdomen with thin red and yellow stripes; tail fan and last two segments of abdomen transparent. Rostrum short, reaching the end of the eye and usually having a single ventral tooth near the tip. *Size*: To 25 mm (1 in). *Range*: Ucluelet, British Columbia to Morro Bay, California. *Habitat*: Found underneath boulders from the very low intertidal to at least 15 m* (50 ft). *Remarks*: At low tide, large numbers of these small shrimp aggregate wherever the underside of the boulder touches water. Unlike most other intertidal shrimp, they remain clinging to the underside of the rock when it is overturned.

80. *Heptacarpus sitchensis*
Sitka shrimp

Identification: Abdomen usually bright green; carapace sometimes similar but more often with diagonal red lines. Entire shrimp can be virtually transparent when algae is scarce. Rostrum fairly long, about equal in length to the rest of the carapace. *Size*: To 28 mm (1.1 in). *Range*: Resurrection Bay, Alaska to Baja California. *Habitat*: Most abundant on mixed gravel and sand beaches with algae and among eelgrass; also common under rocks at low tide. Found from the middle intertidal to 12 m (40 ft). *Remarks*: Many Puget Sound specimens carry a parasitic isopod that appears as a dark mass under the abdomen, resembling a clutch of eggs. In the southern part of its range this shrimp was formerly known as *H. pictus*.

47

81. *Heptacarpus stimpsoni*

Stimpson's shrimp

Identification: Our only shallow-water *Heptacarpus* having slender, simple dactyls on the walking legs. Rostrum relatively short, reaching to the middle of the antennal scale. Color typically a drab brown or gray, broken by light bands near the posterior edge of most of the abdominal segments. *Size*: To 32 mm (1.2 in). *Range*: Sheep Bay, Alaska to Punta Abreojos, Baja California. *Habitat*: Fairly common subtidally on soft bottoms in Puget Sound and occasionally among eelgrass. Found from the intertidal to 73 m (240 ft). *Remarks*: Although it can sometimes be found clinging to the column of the painted anemone, *Urticina crassicornis*,* most individuals do not appear to be associated with other organisms.

82. *Heptacarpus stylus*

Stiletto Shrimp

Identification: A slender shrimp most easily recognized by the numerous tiny but brilliant blue spots scattered over its carapace and abdomen. Shallow-water specimens are usually kelp-colored or, rarely, transparent with broken red markings, while those in deep water are often a solid bright red that fades to lavender when collected. The rostrum is very long and bladelike, and devoid of dorsal spines over most of its length. *Size*: To 57 mm (2.2 in). *Range*: Chicagof Island, Alaska to Puget Sound. *Habitat*: Most abundant among kelp and other brown algae, but also common in eelgrass and surfgrass. Low intertidal and subtidal to 439 m (1440 ft). *Remarks*: Look for this shrimp on the stipes of bull kelp, perched in a head-down position.

83. *Heptacarpus tridens*

Threespine shrimp

Identification: Rostrum long, bearing only three dorsal teeth that are located right above the eyes; abdomen with a very prominent hump. Color extremely variable depending on habitat. *Size*: To 61 mm (2.4 in). *Range*: Aleutian Islands to Seattle*, Washington. *Habitat*: Common subtidally in Puget Sound in a wide range of habitats, ranging from vertical rock faces and overhangs to fairly soft, muddy bottoms; especially abundant among clusters of the large plumose anemone, *Metridium giganteum*. Low intertidal to 110 m (360 ft). *Remarks*: Specimens from rocky areas can have red markings virtually identical to those of *H. kincaidi* [78], but the rostrum lacks that species' characteristic white midrib.

84. *Heptacarpus tenuissimus*

Slender shrimp

Identification: A delicate, transparent shrimp having a very long rostrum that lacks dorsal teeth on the outer half and with a conspicuous dorsal hump on the abdomen. A continuous line of bright red extends along the entire length of the body, starting from the inner margin of the antennal scale. *Size*: To 43 mm (1.7 in). *Range*: Bird Island, Alaska to Catalina Island, California. Uncommon in Puget Sound. *Habitat*: Shallow water to 137 m (450 ft). Found both on mixed composition bottoms and around mud and eelgrass. *Remarks*: Some *H. stylus* [82] are transparent with similar reddish markings, but the red color does not form an unbroken line as it does in *H. tenuissimus*.

85. *Hippolyte clarki*

Grass shrimp

Identification: Small and slender, with rostrum ascending slightly and ending in three points; carpus of second leg only subdivided into three sections instead of seven. Color usually a bright, uniform green to match its surroundings; brown or reddish specimens also common. *Size*: To 31 mm (1.2 in). *Range*: Sheep Bay, Alaska to Isla Cedros, Baja California. *Habitat*: Found in eelgrass beds and among kelp, from the low intertidal to 30 m (100 ft). *Remarks*: Exceptionally common in eelgrass beds in the northern part of its range. In California it is reported to associate with the giant kelp, *Macrocystis*.

86. *Hippolyte californiensis*

California green shrimp

Identification: Virtually identical to *H. clarki* [85]. The rostrum is straighter and ends in two points instead of three, and the basal segment of the first antennae has one or two spines at the tip instead of none. *Size*: To 40 mm (1.6 in). *Range*: Sheep Bay, Alaska to Baja California. *Habitat*: Found in the eelgrass beds of quiet bays, from the low intertidal to 10 m (33 ft). *Remarks*: Inconspicuous during the daytime but very active at night.

87. *Lebbeus catalepsis*

Cataleptic shrimp

Identification: Rostrum short, composed of a simple spine that does not reach farther forward than the eye; carapace with large curved spines. Color extremely variable, ranging from yellow or brown to purplish pink. Abdomen kept elevated in the "cataleptic" position. **Size**: To 22 mm (0.8 in). **Range**: A recently described species, currently known only from several areas along the Strait of Juan de Fuca in Washington. **Habitat**: Found very low in the intertidal of semiprotected rocky outer coast beaches, clinging tightly to algae and the sides of rocks. **Remarks**: A similar species, *L. lagunae*, occurs from Pacific Grove, California to Isla Cedros, Baja California. The rear margin of the fifth segment of the abdomen has a prominent downward projection on each side, and the dorsal surface of the telson has three pairs of spines instead of two.

88. *Lebbeus grandimanus*

Candy stripe shrimp

Identification: Distinctively marked with brilliant bands of red, yellow, and blue; although there is considerable variation in the intensity, this shrimp cannot be confused with any other species on the Pacific Coast. **Size**: To 45 mm (1.8 in). **Range**: Bering Sea to Puget Sound. **Habitat**: Lives in association with sea anemones on both rocky and soft bottoms, at depths of 6-180 m (20-590 ft). **Remarks**: Although usually associated with the crimson anemone, *Cribrinopsis fernaldi*, this colorful shrimp has also been found clinging to *Urticina (Tealia) piscivora*, *U. crassicornis*, and *U. columbiana**.

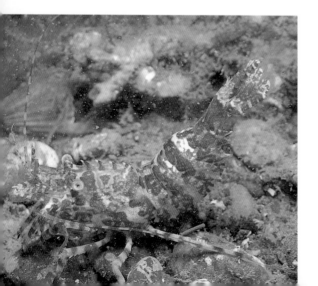

89. *Lebbeus groenlandicus*

Spiny lebbeid

Identification: A stout-bodied shrimp that elevates its spiny abdomen when disturbed. Carapace with four very large teeth; rostrum reaching slightly beyond middle of antennal scale. Typically with brown or reddish-brown bands against a translucent background. **Size**: Rarely to 107 mm (4.2 in); more typically 30-40 mm (1.2-1.6 in). **Range**: Circumboreal, ranging from the Bering Sea to Puget Sound in the eastern Pacific. **Habitat**: Found from the lowest edge of the intertidal (juveniles only) to 518 m (1700 ft), usually where sand or gravel is mixed with shell. **Remarks**: This large and long-lived shrimp makes an excellent addition to a coldwater marine aquarium.

90. *Lysmata californica*

Red rock shrimp

Identification: First pair of antennae unusually long; carpus of second leg subdivided into about 30 articulations. Conspicuously marked with reddish-orange stripes on a translucent background but can change color fairly quickly; sometimes turns pale green at night. *Size*: To about 70 mm (2.7 in). *Range*: Tomales Bay, California to the Galapagos; usually found south of Pt. Conception. *Habitat*: Low intertidal to 60 m (200 ft). Found in tidepools on rocky beaches and in crevices and caves subtidally. Large numbers are sometimes found in association with the California moray; juveniles may hide under sea urchins. *Remarks*: Generally remains under rocks and in crevices during the daytime. Known to act as a 'cleaner' shrimp, removing parasites from fish.

91. *Spirontocaris lamellicornis*

Dana's blade shrimp

Identification: Distinguished by its combination of long, slender, simple dactyls on the walking legs and having nearly the entire dorsal margin of the carapace deeply toothed. Color and pattern extremely variable. *Size*: To 63 mm (2.5 in). *Range*: Bering Sea to Santa Monica Bay, California. *Habitat*: Usually found on sand or muddy bottoms but also occurs in rocky areas; from 3-192 m (10-630 ft). *Remarks*: Symbiotic with sea anemones*, including the crimson anemone *Cribrinopsis fernaldi* and the sand rose anemone *Urticina columbiana*.

92. *Spirontocaris prionota*

Deep blade shrimp

Identification: Blade of rostrum deep, rounded in outline, and armed with very small teeth; carapace spines large and having distinctive serrated margins. Color and pattern extremely variable and can change from day to night. *Size*: To 28 mm (1.1 in). *Range*: Bering Sea to Punta San Carlos, Baja California; also Sea of Japan. *Habitat*: Found subtidally among shell rubble and worm tubes and, less commonly, beneath rocks in the low intertidal. Maximum recorded depth 163 m (534 ft). *Remarks*: This small shrimp is very slow moving and cryptic and may not move even when prodded.

93. *Spirontocaris ochotensis*

Oval blade shrimp

Identification: Rostrum oval in outline and carapace spines confined to anterior half of carapace. Dactyls of walking legs with bifid tips. Color and pattern highly variable. *Size*: To 31 mm (1.2 in). *Range*: Bering Sea to Kyuquot Sound, British Columbia and to Japan in the western Pacific. *Habitat*: Reported from the intertidal zone to 247 m (810 ft). At the Pribilof Islands it appeared to be restricted to rocky areas. *Remarks*: A similar species that also has bifid dactyls, *S. arcuata*, occurs from the Arctic to the San Juan Islands, Washington and also to the Sea of Japan. It can be distinguished from *S. ochotensis* by its carapace spines, the posteriormost being well behind the middle of the carapace.

94. *Spirontocaris snyderi*

Snyder's blade shrimp

Identification: A very slender, diminutive shrimp with three or four dorsal carapace spines that are widely separated from the rostral spines and having simple dactyls on the walking legs. Color usually reddish-brown but variants with all white carapaces or other markings are not uncommon. *Size*: To 24 mm (0.9 in). *Range*: Tasu Sound, British Columbia to Bahia San Cristobal, Baja California. *Habitat*: In Puget Sound this species is symbiotic with the sand rose, anemone, *Urticina columbiana**, which occurs on sand or muddy sand bottoms. Depth range 4-141 m (13-462 ft). *Remarks*: As many as a dozen of these small shrimp can be found on and under a medium sized anemone, usually concealed at the base by the canopy of tentacles and only rarely venturing onto the oral surface.

Family PALAEMONIDAE

95. *Palaemon macrodactylus*

Oriental shrimp

Identification: Claws on second pair of legs larger than first pair; rostrum and carapace with 9 - 15 dorsal teeth, the three posteriormost behind the orbit of the eye. Body usually translucent but sometimes dark green or olive. *Size*: To 58 mm (2.3 in). *Range*: Accidentally introduced from southeast Asia (probably Korea) in the 1950's, this species has become exceptionally abundant in San Francisco Bay and has progressively spread north and south, recently appearing in Willapa Bay, Washington* and also in Malibu Lagoon and Long Beach Harbor, California. *Habitat*: Usually found in estuaries and the brackish waters of tidal creeks. *Remarks*: The use of this shrimp as bait may be partially responsible for accelerating its spread along the Pacific coast.

52

96. *Palaemonella holmesi*

Southern algae shrimp

Identification: Body and appendages transparent; claws on second pair of legs exceptionally long. The rostrum and carapace have 6 - 10 dorsal spines and only two of them are behind the orbit of the eye, and the blade of the antennal scale does not extend beyond the spine. *Size*: To 50 mm (2 in). *Range*: Santa Cruz Island to Ecuador. *Habitat*: Found among algae and shell rubble, from 2-90 m (6-300 ft). *Remarks*: Another small, transparent shrimp, *Palaemon ritteri*, occurs from San Diego to Ecuador and can be found in eelgrass in Mission Bay, California. It has proportionately shorter claws and the blade of the antennal scale extends beyond the spine.

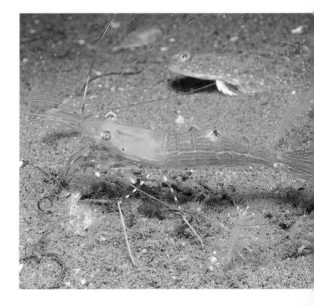

Family PANDALIDAE

97. *Pandalopsis dispar*

Sidestriped shrimp

Identification: Easily differentiated from the genus *Pandalus* by its incredibly long first pair of antennae, which are nearly as long as the entire body. Color pale orange with a long white stripe running the length of the abdomen; irregular, broken markings on abdomen and rear of carapace. *Size*: To 208 mm (8 in). *Range*: Pribilof Islands to Manhattan Beach, Oregon. *Habitat*: Found on soft bottoms in deep water, from 46-649 m (150 - 2128 ft). *Remarks*: Fished commercially with bottom trawls. Because it feeds on smaller crustaceans that it captures in the water column, it is usually not attracted to baited shrimp pots.

98. *Pandalus danae*

Dock shrimp

Identification: Abdomen prominently marked with broken, diagonal stripes that vary from dull brown to red depending on habitat and depth. Legs and antennae strongly banded, and rostrum usually ending in three points. *Size*: To 140 mm (5.5 in). *Range*: Alaskan Peninsula to Point Loma, California. *Habitat*: Most common on mixed composition bottoms, but occurs everywhere from solid rock to silty sand as long as there is some shelter present. Usually remains in crevices and under algae during the day, and is often abundant at night on the pilings of marinas. Ranges from the low intertidal (typically juveniles) to 185 m (606 ft). *Remarks*: This is the pandalid most often seen by divers on our coast, and it forms a part of the sport and commercial shrimp landings. A similar species, *P.gurneyi*, occurs from central California to Bahia San Quintin, Baja California. It has a proportionately longer rostrum and spots instead of stripes on the abdomen.

99. *Pandalus eous*

Alaskan pink shrimp

Identification: A thin-shelled, uniformly pink shrimp with no banding. Middle of third segment of the abdomen with a dorsal spine and spines on the middle posterior margins of the third and fourth segments. *Size*: To 150 mm (5.9 in). *Range*: Bering Sea south to the Washington-Oregon border; Sea of Japan and Korea. *Habitat*: Found on soft bottoms at depths of 16-1380 m (52-4526 ft). *Remarks*: Until recently this was classified as *P. borealis*, a north Atlantic species. It is fished with trawls and is the most economically important shrimp in Alaskan waters. The virtually identical ocean shrimp *P. jordani* lacks the spines on the third and fourth segments of the abdomen; it forms the bulk of the shrimp landings from Washington to California. Both species appear to migrate up into the water column at night to feed on smaller crustaceans.

100. *Pandalus goniurus*

Humpy shrimp

Identification: Carapace pale pink or almost transparent, usually with a thin line starting below the eye, paralleling the lower edge of the carapace, and then curving dorsally. Abdomen with thin red stripes angled upward from front to back; third segment with a distinct dorsal hump that is sometimes formed into a blunt projection. *Size*: To 78 mm (3 in). *Range*: Bering Sea to Puget Sound; also western Pacific to Sea of Japan. *Habitat*: Usually found on mud or sand, from 1*-450 m (3-1476 ft). *Remarks*: These shrimp can be found at night actively scurrying over soft mud bottoms and pouncing on amphipods and other small organisms.

101. *Pandalus hypsinotus*

Coonstriped shrimp

Identification: Carapace with a more arched outline than other pandalids and having more dorsal spines (17-22). Sides of carapace conspicuously marked with bright white spots; legs and antennae strongly banded. Abdomen with wide, irregular reddish bands. *Size*: To 192 mm (7.5 in). *Range*: Norton Sound, Alaska to Puget Sound; also Korea and Japan. *Habitat*: Found on a very wide range of bottom types, at depths from 5-460 m (15-1508 ft). *Remarks*: This species does not seem to occur at high densities like other large pandalids, and is usually caught incidentally with other species in trawls and pots. They are known to feed on mysids and polychaetes in the wild and captive specimens are surprisingly adept at catching smaller shrimp by "caging" them with their walking legs.

102. *Pandalus platyceros*

Spot shrimp

Identification: Our largest shrimp, reddish-brown in color, with characteristic white spots on the first and fifth segments of the abdomen and prominent white stripes on the carapace. Legs and antennae strongly banded. Juveniles in shallow water are sometimes green, brown, or red to match the color of surrounding algae or eelgrass. ***Size***: To 253 mm (9.9 in). ***Range***: Unalaska Island, Alaska to San Diego, California; Sea of Japan and Korea Strait. ***Habitat***: Found on rocky bottoms and vertical rock faces from the very low intertidal (juveniles) to 487 m (1600 ft). ***Remarks***: Supports important sport and commercial pot fisheries. Usually found below normal sport diving depths during the daytime but often encountered at night when they move up to forage in shallow water.

103. *Pandalus stenolepis*

Rough patch shrimp

Identification: Often confused with the dock shrimp *P. danae* [98], being of similar shape and color and having strongly banded appendages. This species is more conspicuously marked with small, bright blue dots than is *P. danae*, and the sides of the abdomen have spots instead of stripes. It can also be distinguished by its narrow antennal scale, in which the spine is wider than the blade at the tip. at the tip. ***Size:*** To 82 mm (3.2 in). in crevices in high scale, in which the spine is wider than the blade ***Range:*** Unalaska, Alaska to Hecata Bank, Oregon. ***Habitat:*** Common in crevices in high current areas as shallow as 6* m (20 ft); found on mud and cobble bottoms in deeper water to 229 m (750 ft). ***Remarks:*** Despite the adult's similarity to other pandalids, the larvae of this species are very distinctive and unmistakable.

Doyne Kessler

104. *Pandalus tridens*

Yellowleg pandalid

Identification: Our only species of *Pandalus* having the combination of banded legs and no stripes or spots on the carapace and abdomen. The last half of the long, slender rostrum is devoid of dorsal spines and ends in three points. ***Size***: Length to 123 mm (4.8 in). ***Range***: Western Bering Sea to San Nicolas Island, California. ***Habitat***: Occurs on both rocky and muddy bottoms, at depths of 5-1984 m (15-6500 ft). ***Remarks***: Sometimes caught in pots along with the spot shrimp *P. platyceros*.

55

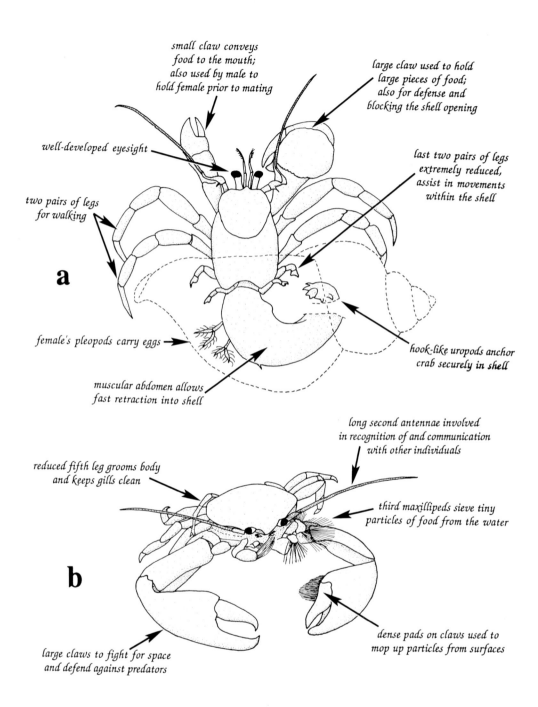

small claw conveys
food to the mouth;
also used by male to
hold female prior to mating

large claw used to hold
large pieces of food;
also for defense and
blocking the shell opening

well-developed eyesight

last two pairs of legs
extremely reduced,
assist in movements
within the shell

two pairs of legs
for walking

a

female's pleopods carry eggs

hook-like uropods anchor
crab securely in shell

muscular abdomen allows
fast retraction into shell

long second antennae involved
in recognition of and communication
with other individuals

reduced fifth leg grooms body
and keeps gills clean

third maxillipeds sieve tiny
particles of food from the water

b

large claws to fight for space
and defend against predators

dense pads on claws used to
mop up particles from surfaces

Figure 8.   (a) hermit crab; (b) porcelain crab.

Anomura

The group known as the Anomura encompasses a wide range of bizarre and interesting decapods, including such familiar ones as the hermit crabs and Alaskan king crabs. Although many bear a strong resemblance to the true crabs or brachyurans, they are easily distinguished by having one pair of antennae outside (lateral to) the eyes and appearing to have only three pairs of walking legs. Anomurans have evolved a wide array of feeding structures and methods and often use their appendages in novel ways; this group includes carnivores, omnivores, filter and deposit feeders, and even some species that are able to use all of these methods.

Ever popular with tide pool visitors, the members of the family **Paguridae** (hermit crabs, pg. 60) provide much entertainment as they busily scour the rocks for scraps of food and scramble about in their perpetual (and often comical) search for the perfect shell. Hermits have soft, unprotected abdomens that are perfectly adapted to fit into the spiral shape of a snail shell, having lost the appendages on the right side of their abdomen so that they fit snugly up against the inner column (Fig. 8a). Even the carapace is largely soft except for a small hardened shield near the front, and they are so dependent on these shelters that a shortage of shells can severely limit populations in a given area. However, the competition for this important resource is not the free-for-all that it sometimes appears to be. Hermits have been playing the shell game since the age of the dinosaurs, and have had plenty of time to develop specific signals to mediate shell exchanges and thus minimize fights and possible injury. Shells are usually acquired through exchanges or recycled as hand-me-downs; although hermits cannot kill snails to acquire shells they are sensitive to the smell of a dead gastropod and those carrying a damaged or poorly-fitting home are especially responsive. Most species show a distinct preference for particular kinds of shells, selecting large, heavy ones into which they can fully retract while others opt for small lightweight models that barely cover their abdomen but allow them greater speed and maneuverability; still others prefer a covering of sponges or stinging hydroids to help deter predators. Those adapted to using worm tubes or tooth shells have straight abdomens but are still missing some right side appendages, suggesting that they descended from more conventional ancestors with coiled abdomens. Such accommodations can have their disadvantages: unlike snail shells, sections of worm tube often have two usable openings and housing shortages sometimes produce crustacean equivalents of the 'pushme-pullyou' of Dr. Doolittle fame.

Hermit crabs are equipped to feed on a wide range of foods. Many spend a great deal of time dredging up sediment with their claws and sorting out organic material with their mouthparts, but they are also able to filter feed with their maxillipeds, scavenge, or prey on smaller organisms. Pagurids are "right handed" in that their right claw is larger and often a much different shape than their left one. Having claws that differ in size, form, and strength probably gives them the flexibility to use a wider range of food resources, but the extremely exaggerated differences often evident in male hermits suggest an even more important role in the competition for mates. Male hermits will drag potential mates around for days while waiting for them to molt, using the small claw to keep a tight grip on the aperture of the female's shell and warding off rival suitors with the large claw.

Not all hermits are created unequal. The **Diogenidae** (pg. 67) share the shell-carrying habit but represent a lineage long separate from the pagurids, and are easily recognized by their equal (or sometimes left-handed) pair of claws. This is primarily a tropical family but there are several species that occur in our region. In addition to using the same feeding methods as the other hermits, some have feathery antennae that are used to filter plankton and detritus from the water.

The north Pacific has by far a greater diversity of **Lithodidae** (pg. 69) than any other part of the world, suggesting that this fascinating group probably evolved in this region. These odd crabs evolved from pagurid hermit crabs and are literally hermits that dropped the habit of carrying shells. Their larvae are almost indistinguishable from those of hermit crabs and as adults they still retain the asymmetry of their ancestors: like pagurids, they are decidedly right-handed and females only have pleopods on the left side of their abdomen. Although most have added at least a few hardened plates for protection, some still have soft, fleshy abdomens loosely folded beneath their bodies that appear every bit as vulnerable as those of hermit crabs. No longer constrained by the size of snail shells, some of the members of this group have attained the greatest size of any crustaceans on our coast, and like their shell-carrying relatives they are equipped to exploit multiple food resources by virtue of having claws of two different shapes and sizes. The fingers of the smaller left claw are spoonlike and close tightly, making it useful for scraping and cropping sessile organisms from the surface of rocks, while the much larger right claw is typically armed with molars for crushing hard-shelled prey. In addition to these tools some of the smaller species have hairs on their maxillipeds for filtering plankton and detritus, thus enabling them to take advantage of a wide range of feeding opportunities. Many of the larger lithodids regularly prey on unpalatable or hard to handle creatures like large starfish or urchins, breaking them apart and ingesting them spines and all. Captive specimens seem to require this excessive calcium in their diet in order to molt properly, and their inability to extract enough of this mineral from sea water might be an evolutionary leftover from their poorly-calcified hermit crab ancestors.

Most lithodids live subtidally in rocky areas where there are fairly strong currents. Although these slow-moving crabs are often brightly colored, they are easily overlooked among the other organisms encrusting the rocks in their habitat. Their unusual carapace shapes and bizarre ornamentation also make them hard to distinguish from their surroundings, and make this group by far the most diverse in form of all the decapod families on our coast.

In sharp contrast, the **Galatheidae** or squat lobsters (pg. 73) vary little in form and, with their crayfish-like bodies and long, slender claws, they are a familiar sight from deep sea submersibles throughout the world. Only two species occur within diving depths along the Pacific coast, and the most famous of these, the pelagic red crab *Pleuroncodes* (commonly called tuna crab or lobster krill) is an infrequent visitor at best. In years when sea surface temperatures are unusually high it sometimes enters inshore waters in phenomenal numbers, with many eventually being cast ashore in windrows along the southern California coast.

Despite having impressively large claws, porcelain crabs (**Porcellanidae**, pg. 74) are harmless filter feeders that strain small particles from the water using their large, fan-like third maxillipeds (Fig. 8b). Much like barnacles, they feed by actively sweeping the water when it is calm and filter passively when there is a current or turbulence, extending their maxillipeds into the flow and periodically cleaning them of accumulated material. Many species also have a large tuft of dense hair on the inside of their claws that works like a dust mop to collect material from the surface of rocks. Porcellanids often have bright coloration on their mouthparts and near the gape of their claws that may serve as a recognition signal during breeding. During courtship a male *Petrolisthes eriomerus* will wave his brilliant blue maxillipeds at a female and display the blue on his claws, while *P. cinctipes* have bright reddish-orange markings in these same places. These two species occur over similar geographic ranges and often on the same beaches, and such color coding may help spare them the wasted time and energy of courting the wrong species. In central California, they share the beach with yet another species, *P. manimaculis*, that has the different combination of blue maxillipeds and red on the claws.

Porcelain crabs are often abundant under rocks and in mussel beds. Many can move rather quickly by pushing off with their claws as they scurry for cover when uncovered and can also swim backwards to a limited extent by flapping their broad abdomens. This group is well known for its propensity to drop off limbs during capture, and when collected should be scooped up from behind to minimize the chances of damage. The zoeal stages of porcellanids are among the most spectacular of decapod larvae (Fig. 9).

Another filter feeder is the sand or mole crab *Emerita analoga* (**Hippidae**, pg. 77), one of only a few large organisms that is adapted to the rigorous habitat of wave-swept sand beaches. These unusual crabs migrate up and down the beach with the tide, maintaining their position in the surf zone and using their second pair of antennae to filter plankton and detritus from the receding waves. The other antennae function as a snorkel and allow the crab to breath when buried in the sand. *Emerita* has one of the greatest distributions of any species on our coast, having been recorded all the way from Alaska to Chile and Argentina. The **Albuneidae** (pg. 77) occur in much the same habitat as *Emerita* and share many of its adaptations to life in shifting sand. In addition to having long, hairy antennae for filtering water, they are also equipped with well-developed claws and adults are believed to be primarily scavengers.

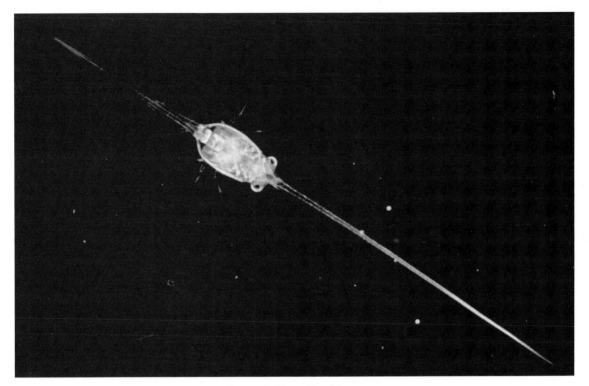

Figure 9. Porcellanid zoea

Family PAGURIDAE

105. *Elassochirus gilli*

Pacific red hermit

Identification: Easily recognized by its brilliant uniform red or orange coloration. The carpus of the large right claw has a smooth surface and is broadly expanded and wider than the hand. *Size*: Carapace length to 38 mm (1.5 in). *Range*: Bering Sea south to Puget Sound in the eastern Pacific and to the Sea of Japan in the west. *Habitat*: Found in areas of bedrock with fairly strong currents, from the low intertidal to 200 m (656 ft). *Remarks*: The color of this attractive hermit resembles that of the brightly colored sea squirts and other organisms found in its habitat.

106. *Elassochirus cavimanus*

Purple hermit

Identification: Nearly identical in form to the Pacific red hermit, *E. gilli*, (except for having small spines on the carpus of the claw) but readily distinguished by its bright purple and yellow claws and white-spotted legs. *Size*: Carapace to 32 mm (1.2 in). *Range*: Bering Sea to Washington. *Habitat*: Found in or close to rocky areas in deep water, from 36-252 m (118-825 ft). *Remarks*: Virtually nothing is known about this species. At the Pribilof Islands it was consistently taken in deeper tows than *E. gilli* and the two were rarely found together, whereas *E. tenuimanus* was common throughout both of their depth ranges.

107. *Elassochirus tenuimanus*

Widehand hermit

Identification: Hand of right claw enormously expanded and flattened, and wider than the carpus. Color reddish brown with purplish-blue on the merus of the walking legs. *Size*: Carapace length to 42 mm (1.6 in). *Range*: Aleutian Islands to Puget Sound. *Habitat*: Low intertidal to 388 m (1272 ft). Occurs on a wide variety of substrates but is most abundant subtidally in well-protected areas with large rock formations. *Remarks*: The large right claw is carried bent underneath the body, and blocks the opening of the shell when the crab retracts.

108. *Labidochirus splendescens*

Splendid hermit

Identification: Our only hermit whose entire carapace is hard. The walking legs are very long and slender and it typically carries a shell just large enough to cover its abdomen. Color brownish-gray to almost pink, with an iridescent sheen on the claws and legs. *Size*: To 28 mm (1.1 in). *Range*: Arctic Ocean south to Puget Sound and the Sea of Japan. *Habitat*: Typically found on open mud or sand bottoms, from 3-412 m (10-1350 ft). *Remarks*: This atypical hermit relies both on its speed and the covering of stinging hydroids on its shell for protection, which have been observed to deter octopuses. In many respects it resembles an evolutionary "missing link" between the hermits and the lithodid crabs.

109. *Haigia diegensis*

Identification: The intense blue color of the third maxillipeds and first pair of antennae make this species easy to separate from the many other small hermits having banded legs. Hand of right claw expanded and much wider than the small claw. *Size*: To at least 13.8 mm (0.5 in). *Range*: Santa Catalina Island, California to Isla Guadalupe, Mexico; primarily around islands but also recorded from the La Jolla area. *Habitat*: Occurs subtidally among boulders and rocks, from 3-18 m (10-60 ft). *Remarks*: Easily overlooked because it is small and lives among rubble piles, and tends to use shells into which it can fully retract.

110. *Phimochirus californiensis*

Identification: Hand of right claw very large, flattened, and mostly white except for some small blue dots. Walking legs and small claw with broad white and reddish-brown bands crossed by darker, lengthwise stripes. Eyestalk orange with blue cornea; antennae banded. *Size*: Carapace to at least 26 mm (1 in). *Range*: Santa Catalina Island, California to Gulf of California. Particularly common around the offshore islands off southern California. *Habitat*: Usually subtidal among rocks or on sand near rocks or other structure, from 10-106 m (30-350 ft). *Remarks*: The flattened right claw is used to seal off the shell opening.

111. *Discorsopagurus schmitti*
Tubeworm hermit

Identification: A tiny hermit with a straight abdomen, usually found in the attached tubes of sabellid or serpulid (calcareous) tubeworms. Right claw only slightly larger than left; legs with reddish-brown bands and fingers of claws yellow or orange. *Size*: To 6 mm (0.2 in). *Range*: Sitka Sound, Alaska to Puget Sound; also Japan. *Habitat*: Primarily on and under large rocks in shallow water and in sabellid worm clusters in deeper water. Can be extremely abundant but overlooked because they quickly retract into their tubes before they are noticed. Occurs from the low intertidal to over 220 m (720 ft). *Remarks*: Females live in attached tubes and are visited by wandering males wearing broken off pieces. This species can filter feed with both the third maxillipeds and antennae, and is also adept at seizing larger pieces of material as it drifts by.

112. *Orthopagurus minimus*
Toothshell hermit

Identification: Like *Discorsopagurus* [111], this small hermit has a straight abdomen and rarely uses snail shells. The flattened right claw is much larger than the left and red except for white teeth on the cutting edges; no banding on legs. *Size*: Small, reaching a carapace length of only 9 mm (0.3 in). *Range*: British Columbia to San Diego; also in the western Pacific. *Habitat*: Strictly subtidal on sand or on rock and shell rubble, from 11-64 m (36-210 ft). *Remarks*: Usually found in tooth shells (*Dentalium*) in the northern part of its range and in broken worm tubes in the south. It characteristically holds the enlarged right claw straight out in front when walking.

113. *Pagurus redondoensis*
Bandclaw hermit

Identification: A tiny hermit with white or pale brown bands on the walking legs but no blue markings near the ends. Claws with a broad, conspicuous white band and narrower dark band on the end of the merus; antennae dark brown with white bands. *Size*: Carapace length to about 6 mm (0.2 in). *Range*: Redondo Beach, California to Baja California Sur, Mexico. *Habitat*: Primarily subtidal among rocks, on pilings, and on clusters of tube mollusks (*Serpulorbis*). Recorded from the intertidal to 50 m (164 ft). *Remarks*: Common, but easily overlooked due to its small size. Often uses the dove shell, *Alia* (*Mitrella*) *carinata*, and sometimes occurs in large aggregations.

62

114. *Pagurus hemphilli*

Maroon hermit

Identification: Easily identified by the distinctive gold rings on the cornea of the eyes. Color a uniform deep red or reddish with white or blue granules; ends of claws and walking legs often light colored. *Size*: Carapace length to 15 mm (0.6 in). *Range*: Klokachef Island, Alaska to Diablo Cove and San Miguel Island, California. *Habitat*: Occurs in the low intertidal but is most abundant on shallow, subtidal rocky bottoms. Limited to areas on or near the open coast. Reported to 50 m (164 ft). *Remarks*: Usually found in top shells or turban shells. Often climbs up into kelp and has been observed perched on the steep sides of rocks, filter feeding in the passing current.

115. *Pagurus stevensae*

Stevens' hermit

Identification: Usually recognized by its habit of wearing a sponge (*Suberites*); however, many specimens carry plain shells and such "hermit sponges" are often appropriated by Bering hermits [122] or other species. The right claw is unusually long and slender and both the claws and walking legs a fairly uniform reddish-brown in color. The antennae are unbanded. *Size*: To 19 mm (0.7 in). *Range*: Akun Island, Bering Sea to Puget Sound. *Habitat*: Subtidal on rocky bottoms from 5*-198 m (15-650 ft). *Remarks*: Although the original snail shell inside the sponge eventually dissolves, the cavity remains and is enlarged as the crab grows.

116. *Pagurus kennerlyi*

Bluespine hermit

Identification: Claws with a dense cover of long, sharp spines that are pale blue to white in color. Antennae distinctly banded; walking legs with reddish-brown blotches and carapace with reddish markings. *Size*: Carapace length to 35 mm (1.4 in). *Range*: Aleutian Islands, Alaska to Puget Sound. *Habitat*: Occurs on a wide range of bottom types, from rock to mud. In the San Juan Islands of Washington it is very common subtidally on slightly silty sand bottoms that are adjacent to large rocks. Recorded from the low intertidal to 274 m (898 ft). *Remarks*: Sometimes uses the hermit sponge (*Suberites*) that is typically inhabited by *P. stevensae* [115].

117. *Pagurus armatus*
Blackeyed hermit

Identification: Easily identified by its large, erect, oval black eyes. Dorsal surface of claws densely covered with spines. Legs and claws with orange banding. *Size*: Carapace length to 43 mm (1.7 in). *Range*: Dutch Harbor, Alaska to San Diego, California. *Habitat*: Found on sand bottoms in sheltered areas, from the low intertidal to 146 m (479 ft). Particularly abundant in sea pen, *Ptilosarcus gurneyi*, beds between 10-20 m (33-65 ft) in Puget Sound. *Remarks*: This is one of the largest and most commonly observed hermits on the Pacific coast, and is almost invariably found inhabiting moon snail (*Polinices* spp.) shells. Small juveniles frequently have shells covered with hydroids, and their corneas are often partly yellow.

118. *Pagurus ochotensis*
Alaskan hermit

Identification: Similar to *P. armatus* [117] in size, habitat, and appearance but easily distinguished by the greenish-yellow corneas of the eyes. The claws have a dark red stripe near the fingers and the dorsal surfaces have granules rather than sharp spines. Legs and claws with an irridescent sheen. *Size*: Large, with carapace length up to 46 mm (1.8 in). *Range*: Pribilof Islands, Alaska to Pt. Arena, California; also to southern Japan. *Habitat*: Found on sand or muddy sand bottoms, from the low intertidal to 388 m (1272 ft). *Remarks*: Like *P. armatus,* it usually inhabits moon snail shells and either one or the other of the two species tends to dominate in a given area. This hermit is far more shy towards divers than is its relative and when approached often runs for several yards before suddenly collapsing and retracting into its shell.

119. *Pagurus spilocarpus*
Spotwrist hermit

Identification: A large, right-handed hermit that is easily recognized by the distinctive shape and color of its eyes and the conspicuous purple coloration on the dorsal surface of the carpus of each claw. *Size*: Carapace length to about 40 mm (1.6 in). *Range*: Zuma Beach, California to Punta Abreojos, Baja California. *Habitat*: Subtidal on quiet, silty sand or gravel to 60 m (197 ft), rarely intertidal. *Remarks*: A fairly recently described species. The common and scientific names both refer to the distinctive purple spot on the carpus of the claw (*spilo* = blotch).

120. *Pagurus samuelis*

Blueband hermit

Identification: A somewhat drab olive green hermit that has very irregular bright blue bands near the end of each walking leg, a striped carapace, and translucent, reddish antennae with no banding. Juveniles conspicuously marked with white bands much like young *P. hirsutiusculus* [125] but can be recognized by their unbanded antennae. *Size*: Carapace length to 19 mm (0.75 in). *Range*: Nootka Sound, British Columbia to Baja California. *Habitat*: Strictly an outer coast species, found in rocky, high intertidal areas. *Remarks*: These active hermits are usually in the shells of black turban snails, *Tegula funebralis*, and tend to tumble from the sides of rocks and tidepools when disturbed. One of the most common and obvious hermits on rocky outer coast beaches from Vancouver Island to California.

121. *Pagurus granosimanus*

Grainyhand hermit

Identification: Color a uniform dark or olive green with white or blue granules, especially on the surface of the claws. Antennae orange, without bands. *Size*: Carapace length to 19 mm (0.7 in). *Range*: Unalaska, Alaska to Ensenada, Baja California. *Habitat*: Common in middle and low intertidal pools and under rocks on protected rocky beaches, though it sometimes occurs in large aggregations on shallow sand bottoms. Recorded to 36 m (118 ft). *Remarks*: Prefers large shells into which it can completely withdraw and that often appear almost too heavy to drag around. Usually found lower on the beach than *P. hirsutiusculus* [125] and higher than *P. beringanus* [122].

122. *Pagurus beringanus*

Bering hermit

Identification: Walking legs pale blue with red spots and bands; claws reddish and densely covered with spines. *Size*: Carapace length to 26 mm (1 in). *Range*: Bering Sea to Monterey, California. *Habitat*: Found from the low intertidal to 364 m (1193 ft). Very common intertidally and subtidally in British Columbia and Washington, especially around large rock formations in protected or semi-protected waters. Primarily subtidal in California and uncommon south of Pt. Arena. *Remarks*: This colorful hermit typically uses the thick, heavy shell of a frilled dogwinkle, *Nucella* (*Thais*) *lamellosa*, into which it can fully retract.

123. *Pagurus caurinus*

Greenmark hermit

Identification: Often mistaken for a small hairy hermit, *P. hirsutiusculus* [125], but can be distinguished from it and the other hermits that have white bands on the legs by its pale orange, unbanded antennae. The claws typically have orangish tips and there are no blue markings on the walking legs. *Size*: To 10 mm (0.4 in). *Range*: Port Gravina, Alaska to San Pedro; rarely reported from California. *Habitat*: Intertidal to 126 m (413 ft). Common in a wide variety of situations ranging from subtidal rocks on or near the exposed open coast to sandy areas in very sheltered waters. *Remarks*: Extremely common and widespread within Puget Sound but most are so small (less than 6 mm (0.2 in) in carapace length) that they are easily overlooked or assumed to be juveniles of other species.

124. *Parapagurodes hartae*

Identification: A very tiny, bright red or orange hermit with patches of brilliant purple on the sides of its claws and legs. The fingers of the small claw are unusually long. *Size:* To about 6 mm (0.2 in). *Range:* Prince William Sound Alaska* to the Mexican border. *Habitat:* Found subtidally on the outer coast from 6-635 m (20-2082 ft) and reported from areas with sand or gravel and broken shell. Large assemblages can be found under boulders in parts of Barkley Sound on Vancouver Island. *Remarks:* This beautiful little hermit is named in honor of the late Josephine F.L. Hart, for her valuable contributions to our knowledge of west coast crustaceans.

125. *Pagurus hirsutiusculus*

Hairy hermit

Identification: This species shows considerable variation in hairiness and its color pattern changes with age. The conspicuous white band at the end of the propodus of the walking legs is a constant feature, and there is usually a bright blue dot at the other end of that segment and blue on the dactyl. Juveniles have several more bright white bands on the claws and legs that darken with age, eventually becoming a fairly uniform olive green to black. Antennae grayish-brown and distinctly banded. *Size*: To 19 mm (0.7 in). *Range*: Pribilof Islands to Monterey, California. *Habitat*: Upper and middle intertidal; rarely subtidal to 110 m (360 ft). *Remarks*: This active hermit uses a small, lightweight shell that it often abandons when handled. It is by far the most common intertidal hermit in Puget Sound and San Francisco Bay. From Monterey to San Diego, California, a very similar species, *P. venturensis*, occurs on sand.

126. *Pagurus retrorsimanus*

Identification: Right claw especially large, bone white in color, and carried bent beneath the body. Walking legs appear light reddish; antennae unbanded and reddish. *Size:* Approximately 15 mm (0.6 in). *Range:* Monterey, California to Los Coronados Islands, Mexico. *Habitat:* Subtidal in rocky areas or on sand between rocks; 11-90 m (36-292 ft). *Remarks:* This interesting species does not appear to be closely related to any of the other west coast hermits.

Mary Wicksten

Family DIOGENIDAE

127. *Isocheles pilosus*

Moonsnail hermit

Identification: Left claw usually slightly larger than right; antennae pale blue and very hairy. Walking legs and claws light yellowish to orange, with blue blotches. *Size*: Carapace length to 30 mm (1.2 in). *Range*: Bodega Bay, California to Baja California. *Habitat*: Found in the sand and mud of bays and estuaries, from the low intertidal to 55m (180 ft). Most common on very shallow subtidal sand bottoms. *Remarks*: Often lives in large aggregations, but is easily overlooked because it spends much of its time buried in sand with only its eyes and antennae exposed. It can filter feed with either its feathery antennae or third maxillipeds and also scavenges.

128. *Paguristes ulreyi*

Furry hermit

Identification: Varies considerably in hairiness and color but easily recognized by its distinctive antennae, which are rather short and stout and have a very conspicuous fringe of long hairs extending from the lower side. Eyestalks very long and slender. Orange to dark brown color often obscured by a thick coat of long, golden hair; mouthparts often with bright white spots. Only the tips of the cutting edges of the claws are black. *Size*: To 22 mm (0.9 in). *Range*: Frederick Island, British Columbia to the Gulf of California. *Habitat*: Intertidal to 157 m (515 ft). Very common in rocky subtidal areas and kelp beds in California, but less conspicuous in the northern part of its range, where it occurs subtidally under boulders and has been reported from intertidal rock crevices on the outer coast of the Queen Charlotte Islands. *Remarks*: The most frequently encountered *Paguristes* on the west coast. The extremely hairy antennae are used for filter feeding.

129. *Paguristes turgidus*

Identification: Claws noticably longer than wide, covered with dark-tipped spines, and with black coloration along at least half the length of the cutting edges. Antennae with only scattered long hairs and no dense fringe. Color a uniform orange or yellow. *Size*: Carapace length to 32 mm (1.3 in). *Range*: Chuckchi Sea to San Diego, California. *Habitat*: Subtidal on muddy sand from 5-465 m (16-1525 ft); also reported from rocky areas. *Remarks*: Specimens from the Pacific Northwest are usually found in shells of the Oregon triton, *Fusitriton oregonensis*.

130. *Paguristes bakeri*

Digger hermit

Identification: Distinguished by the shape of its very hairy and spiny claws, which are almost as wide as they are long. Fixed finger of claw about twice as wide at the base as the moveable finger. Antennae long, slender, and with only sparse hairs; color dark reddish with some blue on walking legs. *Size*: Carapace length to at least 35 mm (1.4 in). *Range*: Bodega Bay, California to Baja and Gulf of California. *Habitat*: Typically subtidal on quiet, silty sand; reported from the low intertidal to 215 m (705 ft). *Remarks*: Buries in sand and can filter feed using its antennae. Usually found in moon snail shells.

131. *Paguristes parvus*

Island hermit

Identification: Surface of claws neither spiny nor hairy. Eyestalks long and slender and distinctly broader at the base than at the tip. Claws creamy white with black tips; walking legs cream with dark brown and red-brown bands. Antennae with brown banding and few hairs. *Size*: To at least 12.7 mm (0.5 in). *Range*: Channel Islands and Palos Verdes Peninsula to Baja California. *Habitat*: Found in the shallow subtidal on the tops of algae-covered rocks, from the low intertidal to 15 m (50 ft). *Remarks*: Common around San Clemente Island, Catalina, and the Channel Islands off California.

Family LITHODIDAE

132. *Acantholithodes hispidus*
Spiny lithode crab

Identification: Carapace and appendages covered with sharp spines tipped with hairs; abdomen soft, pliable, loosely folded under body, and covered with short spines. Claw tips usually a bright reddish-orange. *Size*: Males to 64 mm (2.5 in), females 50 mm (2 in). *Range*: Moorovskoy Bay, Alaska to Monterey and San Nicolas Island, California. *Habitat*: Recorded from the intertidal to 164 m (540 ft) and primarily in deep water in the southern part of its range. Most often found clinging to vertical rock faces in the fjords of southeastern Alaska and British Columbia. *Remarks*: Perceived as a shrimp predator because it occasionally samples the catch in prawn traps, this slow-moving crab is unlikely to ever capture such agile and active prey under natural conditions.

133. *Hapalogaster mertensii*
Hairy crab

Identification: Carapace and claws covered with tufts of long brown hairs. Abdomen very soft and loosely folded under body. Fingers of the claws often reddish orange; large claw with a small, uncalcified opening of unknown function on the underside. *Size*: To 35* mm (1.4 in). *Range*: Atka, Alaska to Puget Sound. *Habitat*: Occurs from the low intertidal to at least 55 m (180 ft). Usually found clinging to the underside of algae-covered rocks that rest on top of other rocks. *Remarks*: This omnivorous crab feeds on smaller animals and algae and can also filter feed. It is largely replaced in the northern part of its range by *H. grebnitzii*, found from the Bering Sea to northern British Columbia and distinguished by its broad, triangular rostrum, the presence of long, slender setae on the inner surface of the large claw, and bluish-black coloration on the fingers of the claw.

134. *Hapalogaster cavicauda*
Furry crab

Identification: Upper surface of carapace, legs, and claws with a plush, velvety covering of short hair; body and appendages flattened and edged with a dense fringe of soft, golden brown hair. Abdomen soft and sack-like, loosely folded under body. *Size*: To 20 mm (0.8 in). *Range*: Cape Mendocino, California to Baja California. *Habitat*: Found under rocks in the low intertidal zone and to 15 m (50 ft). *Remarks*: These odd little crabs cling very tightly to the undersides of rocks, seeming to literally form a slight suction by virtue of the very dense hair fringing their legs and claws. Although capable of filtering to some extent with its maxillipeds, it is by no means limited to filter feeding as has been previously reported and grazes on both plant and animals.

135. *Dermaturus mandtii*

Wrinkled crab

Identification: Claws extremely unequal, with prominent ringlike annulations. Abdomen soft and unsegmented. Color varies from dark grey or brown to white. *Size*: Carapace width to 23 mm (0.9 in). *Range*: Pribilof Islands to Sitka, Alaska; also south to Japan. *Habitat*: Found in rocky areas among kelp holdfasts, in cavities among coralline algae, and in shell rubble at the base of vertical rock faces. Low intertidal to 72 m (236 ft). *Remarks*: Carbon analysis suggests that this species feeds primarily on algae or algal detritus.

136. *Oedignathus inermis*

Granular claw crab

Identification: Carapace somewhat pear-shaped; abdomen very soft and loosely folded under body. Claws grossly unequal in size, the large right one covered with wart-like granules that are blue in adult specimens. *Size*: To 25 mm (1 in). *Range*: Dutch Harbor, Alaska to Pacific Grove, California; western Pacific from Peter the Great Bay to Japan and Korea. *Habitat*: Resides deep in rock crevices, holes, and other secluded locations from the middle intertidal to 15 m (50 ft). Usually limited to areas on or near the outer coast, but can sometimes be found in high current areas within sheltered waters. *Remarks*: Captive specimens are adept at catching worms and crustaceans with their smaller claw and crushing mussels with their large claw; they can also filter feed using the third maxillipeds.

137. *Placetron wosnessenskii*

Scaled crab

Identification: Carapace and legs covered with scale-like plates; claws nearly equal in size and with long, spoonlike fingers. Abdomen of female partially covered with plates; male abdomen soft with vestigial plates. Overall color varies from greenish grey to reddish; walking legs with some banding and yellow and orange near the tips. *Size*: Males and females* to 72 mm (2.9 in). *Range*: Pribilof Islands* to Puget Sound. *Habitat*: Found on vertical rock faces and overhangs associated with large aggregations of plumose anemones (*Metridium*), and also among boulders. Shallow subtidal to 110 m (360 ft), rarely intertidal. *Remarks*: This atypical lithodid is quite fast. The odd claws may be used like forceps to extract prey from crevices; one was seen eating a crevice-dwelling brittle star and, along with brittle star remains, I have found small shrimp, amphipods, crabs, and even a brachiopod in stomach and fecal samples.

70

138. *Cryptolithodes sitchensis*

Umbrella crab

Identification: Carapace expanded laterally to form wing-like projections that conceal the legs when viewed from above. Rostrum distinctly widened at the tip; surface of claws and abdominal plates smooth. Color and pattern extremely variable, ranging from bright red or orange to gray or white. *Size*: To 90 mm (3.6 in). *Range*: Sitka, Alaska to Point Loma, California. *Habitat*: Usually found on bedrock from the low intertidal to 17 m (56 ft) in semi-protected areas on or near the outer coast. *Remarks*: This odd, slow-moving crab can be mistaken for an old clam shell or patch of coralline algae as it grazes on sessile organisms.

a.

139. *Cryptolithodes typicus*

Butterfly crab

Identification: Distinguished from *C. sitchensis* [138] by the roughened surface of its claws, abdominal plates with raised margins, and rostrum that narrows at the tip. Color extremely variable, with central portion often contrasting with "wings", thus resembling a butterfly. *Size*: To 80 mm (3.2 in). *Range*: Amchitka Island, Alaska to Santa Rosa Island, California. *Habitat*: Found from the low intertidal to 45 m (147 ft), often among shell rubble at the base of steep, rocky slopes. Generally found slightly deeper than *C. sitchensis* and not so restricted to the open coast, occurring in high current areas within protected waters. *Remarks*: This small crab blends in well with its surroundings, especially when hiding among the accumulations of old, dead bivalve shells that it often resembles. It grazes on bryozoans, coralline algae, and other attached organisms.

b.

Dan Gotshall

140. *Paralithodes camtschaticus*

Red king crab

Identification: The largest crab on our coast. Carapace, legs and claws covered with thornlike spines that are proportionately longer and sharper in juveniles. Walking legs long. Color ranging from pale brownish red to purple. *Size*: To 280 mm (11 in). *Range*: Bering Sea south to the Queen Charlotte Islands and to Japan in the western Pacific. *Habitat*: Open sand or mud bottoms from 3-366 m (10-1200 ft). Very small juveniles sometimes common intertidally among rocks and algae. *Remarks*: An important commercial species in Alaskan waters. Feeds on a wide range of benthic invertebrates including seastars, urchins, clams, and barnacles. Juveniles form spectacular aggregations or "pods", often in very shallow water, that can contain thousands of individuals. Pods break up shortly after dusk as the members disperse to forage, then re-form just before dawn.

141. *Rhinolithodes wosnessenskii*

Rhinoceros crab

Identification: Carapace triangular in outline with a very deep semicircular depression; claws and legs covered with spines tipped with long hairs. Color usually a light grayish brown except for orange and cream markings in the large carapace depression. *Size*: To 64 mm (2.5 in). *Range*: Kodiak, Alaska to Crescent City, California. *Habitat*: Found on rock or gravel bottoms from 6-73 m (20-240 ft), often residing in crevices. *Remarks*: Sighted very infrequently. It is not known whether this slow-moving crab is truly scarce or just overlooked, because it is very hard to distinguish from all the encrusting organisms found in its natural habitat.

142. *Phyllolithodes papillosus*

Heart crab

Identification: Carapace triangular in outline, with a raised, heart-shaped sculpturing. Claws, legs, and edge of carapace armed with long, flattened projections which are much less developed in juveniles. Color usually grayish or brown; juveniles often white with purple or orange markings. *Size*: To 90 mm (3.6 in). *Range*: Dutch Harbor, Alaska to San Miguel Island, California. *Habitat*: Although juveniles can sometimes be found under rocks at low tide, this species is most often seen subtidally in shallow rocky areas with moderate to strong currents and has been reported to 183 m (600 ft). *Remarks*: Captive specimens are particularly adept at handling and eating small sea urchins, and one specimen was observed feeding on a sponge in the wild.

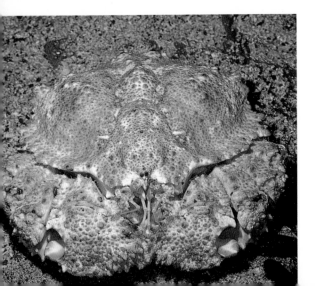

143. *Lopholithodes foraminatus*

Brown box crab

Identification: Similar to *L. mandtii* [144] in shape but lacking its relative's brilliant coloration, being predominantly a drab reddish-brown or tan. Claws and first pair of walking legs each with smooth, semicircular concavities that combine to form a nearly perfectly round opening when folded together. *Size*: To 185 mm (7.4 in), but much larger ones have been reported. *Range*: Kodiak, Alaska to San Diego, California. *Habitat*: Low intertidal to 547 m (1800 ft). Typically found on muddy bottoms below 18 m (60 ft) and occasionally seen on vertical rock faces overlooking soft bottoms. Once considered common in Puget Sound but rarely encountered there in recent years. *Remarks*: Reportedly deposit feeds by filtering sediment dredged up by its claws and also preys on the small clams exposed by its digging. The circular openings in the claws aid in respiration when the crab is buried in the sediment.

144. *Lopholithodes mandtii*

Puget Sound king crab

Identification: Easily recognized by its stout, box-like body and brilliant coloration. Adults red with yellow, orange, and purple markings (especially on the underside); tiny juveniles a uniform bright reddish-orange and with especially prominent cone-like elevations on the carapace. *Size*: Carapace width to 300 mm (12 in) or more. *Range*: Sitka, Alaska to Monterey, California. *Habitat*: Subtidal to 137 m (450 ft) in areas with strong currents; juveniles occasionally found under rocks during extremely low tides. Depth varies with season, with adults concentrating in relatively shallow water during the late winter and spring to breed. *Remarks*: One of the largest crabs on our coast. Feeds on sea urchins and other echinoderms and has also been observed eating sea anemones.

juvenile

adult

Family GALATHEIDAE

145. *Munida quadrispina*

Squat lobster

Identification: Claws long, slender, and very spiny; edge of carapace with a series of small spines. Color reddish-brown to orange. *Size*: Carapace to 67 mm (2.7 in); typically to 40 mm (1.6 in). *Range*: Sitka, Alaska to Los Coronados, Baja California. *Habitat*: Found from 12*-1463 m (40-4800 ft). Usually seen on rock faces or cobble in low current, slightly silty areas. High densities have been observed from submersibles, clinging to vertical rock faces in areas with extremely low oxygen. *Remarks*: Due to its habit of eating dead or moribund tankmates, *Munida* has garnered an undeserved reputation as a shrimp predator when in fact its diet consists primarily of detritus and small planktonic organisms. On one occasion I encountered large numbers of adults swimming several feet above the bottom, in much the same manner that *Pleuroncodes* [146] maintains its position in the water column.

73

146. *Pleuroncodes planipes*

Pelagic red crab

Identification: Claws much shorter and stouter than those of *Munida* [145] and not obviously spiny. Color reddish. **Size**: Carapace length to 50 mm (2 in). **Range**: Distribution is centered off the west coast of Baja California, but sometimes carried as far north as San Francisco. **Habitat**: Normally found on sand and mud bottoms at depths of 45-90 m (148-295 ft), and also free-swimming in the water column. Occasionally large numbers are carried inshore along the southern California coast, eventually becoming stranded on beaches. **Remarks**: Feeds on copepods and other small organisms in the water column and is itself an important food for many fish and marine mammals.

Family PORCELLANIDAE
147. *Pachycheles rudis*

Thickclaw porcelain crab

Identification: Claws large, unequal, roughened with tubercles, and with a scattered covering of long hairs. Telson composed of five plates. Color variable, often a mottled mix of gray, brown, or white; some (especially juveniles) almost completely white. **Size**: To 19 mm (0.75 in). **Range**: Kodiak, Alaska to Bahia Magdalena, Baja California. **Habitat**: Low intertidal to 29 m (95 ft), under rocks or nestling in holes, holdfasts of kelp, or empty giant barnacle shells. **Remarks**: Equal-sized males and females live together in pairs, often sharing their space with the fuzzy hooded shrimp, *Betaeus setosus* [68]. Found only in areas with good water circulation, it is strictly a filter feeder that fans plankton and detritus from the water using its feathery mouthparts.

148. *Pachycheles pubescens*

Pubescent porcelain crab

Identification: Surface of claws covered with a dense layer of short, thick, brown hair giving them an almost muddy appearance. Rostrum also hairy and sharply pointed. Telson composed of seven plates but asymmetrical patterns of six plates are not infrequent. Color usually reddish brown or orange-brown. **Size**: To 22 mm* (0.9 in). **Range**: Queen Charlotte Islands to Cabo Thurloe, Baja California. **Habitat**: Found under rocks on the open coast and in protected inshore waters in areas with fairly strong currents, from the low intertidal to 55m (180 ft). In Puget Sound it is usually subtidal while *P. rudis* is predominantly intertidal. **Remarks**: A third species, *P. holocericus*, often occurs in sponges from Santa Barbara, California to Bahia Magdalena, Baja California. It has a similar coat of hair on its claws, but the telson is composed of only five plates and the carpus of the claw has a prominent row of tubercles on the dorsal surface.

149. *Petrolisthes cinctipes*

Flat porcelain crab

Identification: Maxillipeds and spot at the base of movable finger of claw reddish-orange; carpus of claw very broad, devoid of hairs and with a distinct lobe on the anterior margin. Walking legs with uncalcified 'windows' on ventral face of merus. Color light to dark brown, occasionally blue; antennae dark red. *Size*: To 24 mm (0.9 in). *Range*: Porcher Island, British Columbia to Santa Barbara, California. *Habitat*: Under rocks in the upper and middle intertidal of beaches on or near the outer coast. Often extremely abundant in beds of the California sea mussel (*Mytilus californianus*). *Remarks*: Although competitively superior to *P. eriomerus* [150], this species avoids rocks that rest on sand or other fine sediments, so tends to be restricted to the upper levels of beaches.

150. *Petrolisthes eriomerus*

Flattop crab

Identification: Maxillipeds bright blue, as is the spot at the base of the moveable finger of the claw when it is opened. Carpus of claw about twice as long as wide, with parallel margins. Color dark brown to blue. *Size*: To 19 mm (0.7 in). *Range*: Chicagof Island, Alaska to La Jolla, California. *Habitat*: Found under rocks from the low intertidal to 86 m (282 ft). Occurs both on exposed coastlines and in calm, sheltered waters. *Remarks*: Strictly limited to the low intertidal because it cannot withstand prolonged exposure to warm temperatures while exposed to the air. In addition to filter feeding, it emerges from hiding at night and uses the large tufts of hair on its claws like dust mops to gather material from the surfaces of rocks.

151. *Petrolisthes manimaculis*

Chocolate porcelain crab

Identification: Similar to *P. eriomerus* [150] in having long, slender claws and bright blue maxillipeds, but can be distinguished by the reddish color at the base of the moveable finger of the claws. Carpus of claw very narrow, 2.4 - 3 times longer than wide. Color usually brown with a characteristic line of small blue dots on the dorsal surface of the claw. *Size*: To 20 mm (0.8 in). *Range*: Bodega Bay, California to Punta Eugenia, Baja California. *Habitat*: Found under rocks in the low intertidal, usually at lower levels than *P. eriomerus*. *Remarks*: Like *P. eriomerus*, these are often difficult to handle, being far more inclined both to pinch and drop off limbs than are *P. cinctipes* [149].

152. *Petrolisthes rathbunae*

Rathbun's porcelain crab

Identification: Carapace prominently adorned with hairy, scalelike striations; legs noticably hairy along their entire length. Color greenish with purple spotting and red banding on legs; maxillipeds and fingers of claws red. *Size*: Carapace width to 19 mm (0.7 in). *Range*: Monterey, California to Isla Guadalupe, Baja California. *Habitat*: Occasionally found under rocks in the low intertidal, but probably more common among shallow, subtidal rock piles. *Remarks*: This crab is extremely difficult to catch underwater because it retreats with such speed and agility into the recesses of its rock pile when disturbed.

153. *Petrolisthes cabrilloi*

Cabrillo's porcelain crab

Identification: Most easily distinguished from *P. cinctipes* [149] (which has identical maxilliped and claw coloration) by the dense covering of hair on the carpus of the claws and along the length of the walking legs, both of which are best seen while the crab is immersed. The carpus of the claw is also proportionately narrower. Color typically light brown. *Size*: To 16 mm (0.6 in). *Range*: Morro Bay, California to Baja California. *Habitat*: Found throughout the intertidal zone, under rocks and in mussel beds. *Remarks*: Both in appearance and habitat, this is a southern California replacement for *P. cinctipes*, a species with which it has often been confused. It is much more tolerant of quiet water and silty conditions than is its northern relative.

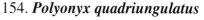

154. *Polyonyx quadriungulatus*

Western tube crab

Identification: Carapace distinctly broader than long. Claws large and slightly unequal, with unusual outward-curving fingers and a dense fringe of hair along the outer margin. *Size*: To 15.5 mm (0.6 in). *Range*: Santa Rosa Island, California to Punta San Eugenio, Baja California. May be largely or wholly limited to offshore islands within U.S. waters. *Habitat*: Sexual pairs reside in the parchment-like tubes of the polychaete *Chaetopterus variopedatus*, typically in sand or mud from the low intertidal to 46 m (150 ft). *Polyonyx* has rarely been found in the intertidal but is very common subtidally at Catalina Island. *Remarks*: These small crabs actively filter feed within the shelter of the worm tube, often creating additional turbulance by flapping their broad abdomens.

Family HIPPIDAE

155. *Emerita analoga*
Pacific sand crab

Identification: Easily distinguished by its smooth, egg-shaped body and flattened legs with no claws. Color usually gray. *Size*: Carapace length to 35 mm (1.4 in). *Range*: Although recorded from Kodiak, Alaska to Chile, it is only occasionally found north of Oregon. Northern populations are derived from larvae carried up the coast which survive but apparently fail to successfully reproduce and do not persist. *Habitat*: Found only on wave-swept sandy beaches, where they remain in the surf zone by moving up and down the beach with the tide. *Remarks*: Filter feeds on plankton and detritus with long, feathery antennae that fold out of sight when not in use. An important prey species for fish and birds and a popular bait with surf fisherman.

Family ALBUNEIDAE

156. *Blepharipoda occidentalis*
Spiny mole crab

Identification: Carapace with four sharp spines on each side, claws spiny. Walking legs flattened, with sickle-shaped tips. *Size*: Carapace length to 60 mm (2.4 in). *Range*: Stinson Beach, California to Baja California. *Habitat*: Found on open sand beaches from the low intertidal to 9 m (30 ft). Does not migrate with the tide. *Remarks*: Usually only molts are seen. These crabs are difficult to spot in the wild because they remain buried with only the tiny eyes exposed and first pair of antennae lying flat on the surface of the sand and quickly sink from sight at the slightest disturbance. Adults are reportedly scavengers (primarily on dead *Emerita* [155]), while juveniles use their feathery antennae to filter feed.

Jenifer Dugan & David Hubbard

157. *Lepidopa californica*
California mole crab

Identification: Similar to the spiny mole crab *Blepharipoda* [156] but lacks spines on the claws and has only one spine on each side of the carapace. Color white with an iridescent sheen. *Size*: Carapace length to 20 mm (0.8 in). *Range*: Monterey to the Gulf of California; usually south of San Pedro. *Habitat*: Found in the very low intertidal of sheltered and open sand beaches and subtidally on sand to 24 m (80 ft), exceptionally to 128 m (425 ft). *Remarks*: Can tolerate much quieter areas than the spiny sand crab. Buries very deeply in the sediment, with the long antennae combining to form a snorkle for respiration.

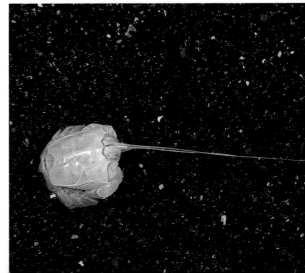

THALASSINIDEA

158. *Neotrypaea californiensis*

Bay ghost shrimp

Identification: Body poorly calcified. Claws unequal, especially in adult males, with a conspicuous gape. Tip of eyestalks pointed. Claw white; body with overall orange, pink, or yellowish cast. ***Size***: To 120 mm (4.8 in). ***Range***: Mutiny Bay, Alaska to Estero Punta Banda, Baja California. ***Habitat***: Sand and muddy sand of bays and estuaries, where it creates multi-branching, impermanent burrows in the middle to low intertidal. ***Remarks***: Feeds on organic material sorted from the sediment as it burrows and also filters the water forced through its burrow by its pleopods. Along with *Upogebia* [160], it is considered a pest on oyster beds, because their burrowing activities can smother or bury oysters. Prized as bait and commercially harvested in some areas. A second species, *N. gigas*, occurs in similar habitats and also subtidally to 50 m (164 ft). It has a sharp rostrum and adult males have extremely long, narrow claws that barely gape when closed.

159. *Neotrypaea affinis*

Tidepool ghost shrimp

Identification: Similar to the bay ghost shrimp, *N. californiensis* [158], but proportionately more slender and has the tips of the eyestalks rounded. Color white. ***Size***: To 65 mm (2.6 in). ***Range***: Cayucos*, California to Bahia San Quintin, Baja California. ***Habitat***: Builds permanent burrows in sandy gravel between and beneath boulders in the middle intertidal zone of protected outer coast beaches. ***Remarks***: This species typically lives in male/female pairs along with a pair of blind gobies, *Typhlogobius californiensis*.

160. *Upogebia pugettensis*

Blue mud shrimp

Identification: Rostrum prominent, covered with short hair. Claws and walking legs very hairy; claws equal in size. Color gray or white to blue. ***Size***: To 150 mm (6 in). ***Range***: Valdez Narrows, Alaska to Morro Bay, California. ***Habitat***: Builds permanent, Y-shaped burrows in low intertidal mud or muddy sand; also present (at much lower densities) on rocky beaches. ***Remarks***: Uses its pleopods to circulate water which it filters for plankton and detritus. Pairs of shrimp frequently share their quarters with *Betaeus harrimani* [67], *Scleroplax granulata* [40], and the arrow goby, *Clevelandia ios*. A clam, *Psuedopythina compressa*, is often found attached to the shrimp's pleopods. South of Newport Bay the common intertidal species is the nearly identical *U. macginitieorum*.

PALINURA

161. *Panulirus interruptus*
California spiny lobster

Identification: Antennae extremely long, stout, and spiny; all appendages lacking claws. Carapace with large, curved spines above each eye. *Size*: Total length to 600 mm (24 in). *Range*: San Luis Obispo County, California to Bahia Rosalia, Baja California. *Habitat*: Found in rocky areas, sheltering under rocks and in crevices and caves during the day and emerging at night. Low intertidal to 60 m (200 ft). *Remarks*: Even though they lack claws, spiny lobsters are remarkably effective predators on a wide range of hard-shelled prey, which are crushed and broken with the powerful mandibles.

Marc Chamberlain

PENAEOIDEA

162. *Penaeus californicus*
Brown shrimp

Identification: First three pairs of legs all with claws; fourth, fifth, and sixth segments of abdomen with a dorsal ridge. Body a uniform brown; legs and pleopods yellowish. *Size*: To 250 mm (10 in). *Range*: San Francisco Bay to Callao, Peru and the Galapagos. *Habitat*: Found on mud and sand from 3*-100 m (10-328 ft); usually 25-50 m (80-164 ft). *Remarks*: An important and widely exported commercial species in Mexico. A related species, *Sicyonia ingentis*, occurs from Monterey Bay south at depths of 5-300 m (15-984 ft) and is also taken commercially. It has a very heavy, thick shell and the dorsal ridge extends along the entire length of the abdomen.

© Norbert Wu

STOMATOPODA

163. *Hemisquilla ensigera californiensis*
Mantis shrimp

Identification: Carapace very small and eyes large; dactyl of large subchelate claw lacking spines. Legs, pleopods, and uropods bright blue. *Size*: To 300 mm (12 in). *Range*: Pt. Conception, California to the Gulf of California and Panama. *Habitat*: Subtidal to 90 m (295 ft) on mud or sand and shell, where it digs burrows up to 2 m (6.5 ft) deep. *Remarks*: Emerges at night to prey on bivalves and other organisms that are smashed by blows from the claws. Great care should be taken when handling these animals because their claws can inflict serious damage. The other species of stomatopods occuring in California can be distinguished by the number of spines on the dactyl: *Pseudosquilla marmorata* (3); *Schmittius politus* (4), and *Nannosquilla anomala* (10-14 spines).

79

GLOSSARY

amphipod- type of small crustacean; familiar examples are sand fleas.

bifid dactyl- a dactyl that splits at the tip, ending in two points.

biramous- refers to an appendage that splits at the base, e.g., antennae, pleopods, uropods.

bivalve- mollusk with two shells, e.g., clams, mussels, oysters, etc.

bryozoan- a type of small, filter-feeding, colonial organism.

carapace- the 'shield' or 'back shell' of a crab or shrimp, covering the head and thorax.

carpus- the "wrist" of a crustacean limb; the third segment in from the end.

cataleptic position- defensive position assumed by some shrimp in which the tail is elevated towards the head.

commensal- relationship where organisms of different species live together, with one benefiting while the other neither benefits nor is harmed.

copepod- a type of tiny, planktonic crustacean.

coralline algae- a very hard, encrusting algae often forming a purplish-pink coating on rocks.

cornea- the faceted part of the eye.

dactyl- the last segment of the typically seven-segmented crustacean limb.

detritus- small particles of decomposing plant and animal material, often rich in bacteria.

diatoms- single-celled, often planktonic, photosynthetic organisms that form much of the base of the food chain in marine systems.

eelgrass- a rooted, flowering plant that often forms dense beds in shallow sandy or muddy areas.

echinoderm- refers to the group that includes starfish, sea urchins, brittle stars, and sea cucumbers.

El Niño- an oceanographic condition that results in unusually warm water along the Pacific coast.

estuarine- refers to the area where freshwater meets saltwater, such as at the mouth of rivers.

exopod- the lateral (outside) branch of a *biramous* appendage.

filter-feeding- feeding by straining small particles out of the water.

holdfast- the rootlike structure that algae use to adhere to the substrate.

intertidal- the area exposed at low tide.

maxilliped- a thoracic appendage that functions as a mouthpart.

megalops- the final larval form of a decapod; swims by using *pleopods*.

merus- the fourth segment from the end of a crustacean limb, usually the longest of the segments.

mysid- a type of small, shrimplike crustacean that often forms schools in the water column.

planktonic- refers to organisms floating freely in the water column.

pleopod- paired appendages associated with the abdominal segments, used for brooding eggs and by shrimps for forward swimming (swimmerets).

polychaete- member of a very large and diverse group of segmented marine worms.

pot- baited trap used to catch shrimp and crab.

propodus- the next-to-last segment of a crustacean appendage; forms the 'hand" of the clawed appendage.

rostrum- anterior projection of the carapace between the eyes.

sessile- refers to organisms that are permanently attached to the bottom.

stipe- the "stalk" of an alga.

subtidal- area below the level of the lowest tides.

telson- the last section of a crustacean's abdomen; bears the anus.

trawl- type of net that is dragged behind a boat.

tubercles- rounded bumps or projections.

uropod- paired appendages associated with the last (sixth) segment of the abdomen; combines with the telson to form the tail fan.

zoea- larval stage of a crustacean, followed by the *megalops* stage.

SELECTED REFERENCES

Butler, T.H. 1980. Shrimps of the Pacific Coast of Canada. Can. Bull. Fish. Aquat. Sci. No. 202. 280 pp.

Garth, J.S. 1958. Brachyura of the Pacific coast of America. Oxyrhyncha. Allan Hancock Pacific Exped. 21: 1-854.

Haig, J. 1960. The Porcellanidae (Crustacea Anomura) of the eastern Pacific. Allan Hancock Pacific Exped. 24: 1-440.

Hart, J.F.L. 1964. Shrimps of the genus *Betaeus* on the Pacific coast of North America with descriptions of three new species. Proc. U.S. Nat. Mus. 115: 431-466.

_____ 1982. Crabs and their relatives of British Columbia. Handbook 40. British Columbia Provincial Museum, Victoria, British Columbia. 267 pp.

Hiatt, R.W. 1948. The biology of the lined shore crab, *Pachygrapsus crassipes* Randall. Pacific Sci. 2: 135-213.

Hines, A.H. 1982. Coexistence in a kelp forest: size, population dynamics, and resource partitioning in a guild of spider crabs (Brachyura: Majidae). Ecol. Monogr. 52: 179-198.

Jensen, G.C. 1989. Gregarious settlement by megalopae of the porcelain crabs *Petrolisthes cinctipes* (Randall) and *P. eriomerus* Stimpson. J. exp. mar. Biol. Ecol. 131: 223-231.

_____ and D.A. Armstrong. 1991. Intertidal zonation among congeners: factors regulating distribution of porcelain crabs *Petrolisthes* spp. (Anomura: Porcellanidae). Mar. Ecol. Prog. Ser. 73: 47-60.

Johnson, M.E., and H.J. Snook. 1927. Seashore animals of the Pacific coast. New York: Macmillan (Paperback ed., Dover, New York, 1967.)

Kessler, D.W. 1985. Alaska's saltwater fishes and other sea life: a field guide. Alaska Northwest Publishing Co., Anchorage, Alaska. 358 pp.

Knudson, J.W. 1964. Observations of the reproductive cycles and ecology of the common Brachyura and crablike Anomura of Puget Sound, Washington. Pacific Sci. 18: 3-33.

MacGinnitie, G.E., and N. MacGinnitie. 1968. Natural history of marine animals. 2nd ed., rev. New York: McGraw-Hill. 523 pp.

McLaughlin, P.A. 1974. The hermit crabs (Crustacea Decapoda, Paguridea) of northwestern North America. Zool. Verh. Leiden 130: 1-396.

Morris, R.H., D.P. Abbott, and E.C. Haderlie, eds. 1980. Intertidal invertebrates of California. Stanford Univ. Press, Stanford. 690 pp.

Pearce, J.B. 1966. The biology of the mussel crab, *Fabia subquadrata*, from the waters of the San Juan Archipelago, Washington. Pacific Sci. 20: 3-35.

Rathbun, M.J. 1904. Decapod crustaceans of the northwest coast of North America. Harriman Alaska Expedition 10: 1-210.

_____ 1918. The grapsoid crabs of America. Bull. U.S. Nat. Mus. 97: 1-461.

_____ 1925. The spider crabs of America. Bull. U.S. Nat. Mus. 129: 1-613.

_____ 1930. The cancroid crabs of America. Bull. U.S. Nat. Mus. 152: 1-609.

Ricketts, E.F. and J. Calvin. 1968. Between Pacific tides. 4th ed. Revised by J.W. Hedgpeth. Stanford, Calif.: Stanford University Press. 614 pp.

Schmitt, W.L. 1921. The marine decapod Crustacea of California. Univ. Calif. Publ. Zool. 23: 1-470.

Smith, R.I., and J.T. Carlton (editors) 1975. Light's manual: intertidal invertebrates of the central California coast. Third ed. Univ. of Calif. Press, Berkeley. 716 pp.

Wicksten, M.K. 1977. Artificial key to shallow-water hermit crabs of California. Proceedings of the taxonomic standardization program, Southern California Coastal Water Research Project, El Segundo. Vol. 5: 23-28.

_____ 1979. Decorating behavior in *Loxorhynchus crispatus* Stimpson and *Loxorhynchus grandis* Stimpson (Brachyura, Majidae). Crustaceana, (suppl.) 5: 37-46.

_____ 1980. Decorator crabs. Sci. American 242: 116-122.

_____ 1989. A key to the palaemonid shrimp of the eastern Pacific region. Bull. So. Calif. Acad. Sci. 88: 11-20.

_____1990. Key to the hippolytid shrimp of the eastern Pacific Ocean. Fish. Bull., U.S. 88: 587-598.

Williams, A.B. 1986. Mud shrimps, *Upogebia*, from the eastern Pacific (Thalassinoidea: Upogebiidae). Memoir of the San Diego Society of Natural History, no. 14. 60 pp.

_____, L.G. Abele, D.L. Felder, H.H. Hobbs, Jr., R.B. Manning, P.A. McLaughlin, and I.P. Farfante. 1989. Common and scientific names of aquatic invertebrates from the United States and Canada: decapod crustaceans. American Fisheries Soc. Spec. Pub. 17. 77 pp.

Zmarzly, D.L. 1992. Taxonomic review of pea crabs in the genus *Pinnixa* (Decapoda: Brachyura: Pinnotheridae) occurring on the California shelf, with descriptions of two new species. J. Crustacean Biol. 12: 677-713.

INDEX

Species numbers are in brackets.

SPECIES CHECKLIST

Nannosquilla anomala
Neotrypaea affinis
Neotrypaea californiensis
Neotrypaea gigas
Oedignathus inermis
Opisthopus transversus
Oregonia gracilis
Orthopagurus tenuis
Pachycheles holosericus
Pachycheles pubescens
Pachycheles rudis
Pachygrapsus crassipes
Paguristes bakeri
Paguristes parvus
Paguristes turgidus
Paguristes ulryi
Pagurus armatus
Pagurus beringanus
Pagurus caurinus
Pagurus granosimanus
Pagurus hemphilli
Pagurus hirsutiusculus
Pagurus kennerlyi
Pagurus ochotensis
Pagurus redondoensis
Pagurus samuelis
Pagurus spilocarpus
Pagurus spp. 1
Pagurus spp. 2
Pagurus stevensae
Pagurus venturensis
Palaemon macrodactylus
Palaemon ritteri
Palaemonella holmesi
Pandalopsis dispar
Pandalus danae
Pandalus eous
Pandalus goniurus
Pandalus hypsinotus
Pandalus jordani
Pandalus platyceros
Pandalus stenolepis
Pandalus tridens
Panulirus interruptus
Paracrangon echinata
Paralithodes camtschaticus
Paraxanthias taylori
Pelia tumida

Penaeus californicus
Petrolisthes cabrilloi
Petrolisthes cinctipes
Petrolisthes eriomerus
Petrolisthes manimaculis
Petrolisthes rathbunae
Phimochirus californiensis
Phyllolithodes papillosus
Pilumnus spinohirsutus
Pinnixa barnharti
Pinnixa faba
Pinnixa littoralis
Pinnixa tubicola
Pinnotheres pugettensis
Pinnotheres taylori
Placetron wossnessenskii
Pleuroncodes planipes
Podochela hemphilli
Polyonyx quadriungulatus
Portunus xantusii
Pugettia dalli
Pugettia gracilis
Pugettia producta
Pugettia richii
Pyromaia tuberculatus
Randallia ornata
Rhinolithodes wossnessenskii
Rhynocrangon alata
Rithropanopeus harrisii
Sclerocrangon boreas
Scleroplax granulata
Scyra acutifrons
Sicyonia ingentis
Spirontocaris arcuatus
Spirontocaris lamellicornis
Spirontocaris ochotensis
Spirontocaris prionota
Spirontocaris snyderi
Synalpheus lockingtoni
Taliepus nuttallii
Telmessus cheiragonus
Uca crenulata
Upogebia pugettensis
Upogebia macginiteorum